Universal Verification Methodology Based Verification Environment

Abhishek Jain

Universal Verification Methodology Based Verification Environment

Theory and Practice

LAP LAMBERT Academic Publishing

Impressum / Imprint
Bibliografische Information der Deutschen Nationalbibliothek: Die Deutsche Nationalbibliothek verzeichnet diese Publikation in der Deutschen Nationalbibliografie; detaillierte bibliografische Daten sind im Internet über http://dnb.d-nb.de abrufbar.
Alle in diesem Buch genannten Marken und Produktnamen unterliegen warenzeichen-, marken- oder patentrechtlichem Schutz bzw. sind Warenzeichen oder eingetragene Warenzeichen der jeweiligen Inhaber. Die Wiedergabe von Marken, Produktnamen, Gebrauchsnamen, Handelsnamen, Warenbezeichnungen u.s.w. in diesem Werk berechtigt auch ohne besondere Kennzeichnung nicht zu der Annahme, dass solche Namen im Sinne der Warenzeichen- und Markenschutzgesetzgebung als frei zu betrachten wären und daher von jedermann benutzt werden dürften.

Bibliographic information published by the Deutsche Nationalbibliothek: The Deutsche Nationalbibliothek lists this publication in the Deutsche Nationalbibliografie; detailed bibliographic data are available in the Internet at http://dnb.d-nb.de.
Any brand names and product names mentioned in this book are subject to trademark, brand or patent protection and are trademarks or registered trademarks of their respective holders. The use of brand names, product names, common names, trade names, product descriptions etc. even without a particular marking in this works is in no way to be construed to mean that such names may be regarded as unrestricted in respect of trademark and brand protection legislation and could thus be used by anyone.

Coverbild / Cover image: www.ingimage.com

Verlag / Publisher:
LAP LAMBERT Academic Publishing
ist ein Imprint der / is a trademark of
OmniScriptum GmbH & Co. KG
Heinrich-Böcking-Str. 6-8, 66121 Saarbrücken, Deutschland / Germany
Email: info@lap-publishing.com

Herstellung: siehe letzte Seite /
Printed at: see last page
ISBN: 978-3-659-47604-4

Table of Contents

LIST OF FIGURES

PREFACE

This book covers the concepts of Universal Verification Methodology (UVM) and practical usage of UVM for developing Advanced Verification Environments at all levels.

In this first edition of book *Universal Verification Methodology based Verification Environment – Theory and Practice,* Generic and Reusable Universal Verification Methodology (UVM) based Verification Environments for efficient verification of Imaging Sensor/Coprocessor designs is described. This book is written primarily for verification engineers performing verification of complex IP blocks or entire system-on-chip (SoC) designs. However, much of material will also be of interest to SoC project managers as well as designers to learn more about verification. This book describes very useful information about Universal Verification Methodology along with assertion-based verification, hardware emulation or acceleration and Transaction Level Modeling. Furthermore, this book includes detailed information about verification environment for one case which can be easily used as reference for other cases.

This book includes description of efficient and unified verification environment (at IP/Subsystem/SoC Level) which reuses the already developed Verification components and also sequences written at IP/Subsystem level can be reused at SoC Level both with Host BFM and actual Core using Incisive Software Extension (ISX) and Virtual Register Interface (VRI) approaches. IP-XACT based tools are described for automatically configuring the environment for various IPs/SoCs.

The first chapter is devoted to the introduction of the Universal Verification Methodology (UVM) and its main features and advantages. Verification Environment/Methodology used in imaging group in the past and therefore main challenges of previous Verification Environment/Methodology is described. Then, to overcome those challenges, development of Universal Verification Methodology based Verification Environment and its main advantages are described.

Chapter-2 describes possible interfaces of Image Signal Processing IP and main blocks of UVM based IP Level Verification Environment. Next in this unit, UVM test bench architecture is described. Procedure to do synchronization between Register sequences and data sequences is also described. Finally, flow of IP level Verification Environment is described.

Chapter-3 describes main blocks of UVM based Subsystem Level Verification Environment. Finally, reuse of IP level Verification Environment and sequences at Subsystem Level is described.

Chapter-4 describes UVM based SoC Level Verification Environment. Then, two main approaches (ISX and VRI) are described to reuse the IP/Subsystem level verification environment when we replace Host BFM with actual Core.

Chapter-5 begins with description of the SPIRIT and IP-XACT. Then, IP-XACT flow used in imaging group is described. Applications of IP-XACT tools to automatically generate UVM based Verification Environment files are described and at the end; significance of the spirit scripts is described.

Chapter-6 describes main concepts of UVM_REG register and memory model. Next in this unit, usage of UVM_REG register model for programming of registers and memories of designs is described. At the end, built-in sequences of UVM_REG register and memory model is described.

Chapter-7 begins with description of development flow of Image signal processing IP and ISP. Next in this unit, the basic setup of UVM based verification environment using C/Python reference models for IP/Subsystem/SoC level verification is described. Finally, the importance of the usage of reference model for bit accurate verification is described.

Chapter-8 describes the concepts of Assertion Based Verification (ABV) and formal verification. Major applications of Assertion Based VIP in imaging group are also described.

Chapter-9 describes the basics of accelerated VIP. Next in this unit, the concepts of emulation and co-emulation are described. Further in this unit, simulation to emulation implementation with help of sample example code is described. At the end, VRI based Veloce emulation platform is discussed.

Chapter-10 describes the concept of SystemC language for system level modeling and transaction level modeling in detail. Next in this unit, case study of ISP IP is described in detail. Importance of the reuse of ISP TLM model in RTL verification environment is also described. An improved multi-language verification flow is described, by addressing major activities of verification.

Chapter-11 describes the use of Enterprise Manager for running regressions and coverage analysis. Also the internal verification flow for efficient setup of simulations and regressions is described.

Keywords

SystemVerilog, Universal Verification Methodology (UVM), register interface, video data interface, Universal Verification Component (UVC), register and memory model, SPIRIT, IP-XACT, Incisive Software Extension (ISX), Virtual Register Interface (VRI), reference model, Assertion Based VIP, Accelerated VIP, co-emulation, Transaction level modeling, UVM-ML.

ACKNOWLEDGEMENTS

I would have never succeeded in completing my book without the cooperation, encouragement and help provided to me by various people.

Foremost, I would like to express my sincere gratitude to **Dr. Hima Gupta** (Professor, Jaypee Business School, Jaypee Institute of Information Technology), **Giuseppe Bonanno** (CAD Manager, Imaging Division, STMicroelectronics) and **Nikhil Kulshrestha** (Senior Group Manager, Imaging Division, STMicroelectronics) for the continuous support of my Ph.D study and research, for their patience, motivation, enthusiasm, and immense knowledge. Their guidance helped me in all the time of work done and writing of this book.

Besides my advisors, I would like to thank management and team members of Imaging Division, STMicroelectronics; Faculty members and peer scholars of JBS, Jaypee Institute of Information Technology University for their support and guidance.

My sincere thanks also go to **Piyush Kumar Gupta** (Group Manager, SDS Group, STMicroelectronics)**, Sachish Dhar Dwivedi** (Staff Engineer, SDS Group, STMicroelectronics) and **Krishna Kumar** (Staff Engineer, SPG Group, STMicroelectronics) for their significant contribution in chapters on *Accelerated VIP* and *SystemC and Transaction Level Modeling*.

Last but not the least; I would like to thank my family: my parents, my wife **Ekta** and Sons (**Arnav** and **Aryan**) for their patience and support.

- Abhishek Jain

1. Introduction

Structure

1.1 Overview

1.2 Coverage Driven Verification

1.3 Challenges faced and their Solution

1.1 Overview

Universal Verification Methodology (UVM) is the first standard, interoperable, open, and proven verification re-use methodology. It provides interoperability of simulator, verification IP and high-level language within and across companies. It is scalable from IP level to system-level verification. It gives automation feature, which is important for reuse of Verification Environment. It is developed, documented and maintained by multiple vendors and it does not bind users to use single vendor solution like existing class libraries.

UVM is a methodology used for the functional verification of digital hardware, mainly using simulation. The hardware or system which is to be verified would typically be described using VHDL, Verilog, System Verilog or System C at any appropriate abstraction level. This could be register transfer level, behavioral or gate level. Universal Verification Methodology is mainly targeted for simulation but it can also be used along with assertion-based verification and hardware emulation or acceleration.

Objectives

After studying this unit, you will be able to:

- Assess the importance of Universal Verification Methodology.

- Understand coverage-driven verification.

- Evaluate the significance of Generic Universal Verification Methodology based reusable verification environment.

1.2 Coverage Driven Verification

Coverage-driven verification (CDV) can be easily achieved using Universal Verification Methodology (UVM). CDV join together automatic generation of test, self-checking mechanism in test benches, and coverage metrics to reduce the significant time spent verifying a design. The main purpose of CDV is to:

- Remove the effort and time spent in creating thousands of tests.
- Ensure complete verification using target set in advance.
- Receive error notifications early in the design cycle and use effectively run-time error checking to simplify debug process.

An UVM test bench consists of reusable verification environments called verification components. A verification component is a configurable, encapsulated, ready-made, verification environment for a design sub-module, an interface protocol, or a full system. Each verification component follows a standard architecture and composed of entire set of elements for stimulus generation, data/protocol checking, and obtaining coverage information for a specific design or protocol. The verification component is applied to the device under test (DUT) to verify implementation of the protocol or design architecture.

Self-Assessment Questions:

1. Does UVM provide multiple vendor solution?

2. What do you mean by Coverage Driven Verification?

1.3 Applied Research on Verification

In order to sustain competitive advantage over its competitors, it is very important for the organizations to develop and maintain high quality bug free designs. As functional verification takes approximately 70 percent of the hardware's design cycle and therefore, is paramount within the hardware's design cycle, it is very important to continuously improve the efficiency and effectiveness of the verification of the complex design systems.

Research focus

The focus of applied research on Verification in imaging group is to reduce the costs and improve the effectiveness of the verification and validation techniques in development of large-scale, complex design systems. Our approach is largely based on usage of advanced Verification techniques like Universal Verification Methodology (UVM) along with assertion-based verification and hardware emulation or acceleration for efficient verification of complex designs.

We are also focusing on usage of TLM Driven Verification Methodology and leveraging reuse over abstraction levels.

1.4 Challenges faced and their Solution

With the tight schedules on all projects it is important to have a strong verification methodology which contributes to First Silicon Success. Deploy methodologies which enforce full functional coverage and verification of corner cases through pseudo random test scenarios is required. Also, standardization of verification flow is needed.

In the past, "e" (Specman)/Verilog based Verification Environment was used for IP/Subsystem level verification and C/C++/Verilog based Directed Verification Environment was used for SoC Level Verification in imaging group.

Main Challenges of Previous Environment/Verification Methodology were as follows:

1. Reusability
   a. Test cases from IP/Subsystem level could not be reused at SoC Level.
2. Maintainability
   a. Different Verification Environments were used in different IP and SoCs across multiple sites.
3. Significant time was spent in reproducing the issue reported at SoC level at IP/Subsystem level.
4. How to catch bugs early in the design cycle?
5. How to develop Verification Environment of designs early in the design cycle?
6. Verification of registers at SoC level was not efficient and automatic as small change in the register description caused manual rework in the verification environment and test case(s).
7. At SoC level, it was difficult to align design specification with corresponding RTL implementation and verification environment.

To overcome above challenges, Universal Verification Methodology is adopted. The main aim of development of Generic Universal Verification Methodology based reusable verification environment is to –

1) Develop standard unified methodology which is -
   a) Vendor independent
   b) Reusable from IP -> Subsystem -> SoC both with Host BFM and actual Core.
   c) Open
   d) Leveraging Existing Verification Environment

2) Usage of IP-XACT based tools for automatically generating IPs/SoCs dependent files.

3) Usage of Assertion based VIP (ABVIP) for catching bugs early in the design cycle.

4) Usage of Acceleratable UVCs to increase run time performance.

5) Usage of TLM reference model of RTL for developing Verification Environment early in the design cycle.

The following chapters discuss the new Generic Universal Verification Methodology based Reusable Verification Environment.

Self-Assessment Questions:

3. What are the major reasons to switch to UVM?

4. What is the main aim of development of Generic Universal Verification Methodology based reusable verification environment?

---

2. Universal Verification Methodology based Reusable IP Level Verification Environment

Structure

2.1 Introduction

IP level verification is key aspect in SoC level verification as at SoC level, each IP is a black box and is considered as a golden block. Extensive and thorough IP verification is a key requirement from protocol and functionality perspective. It is essential to verify each and every feature of IP to greatest extent possible and delivering a zero bug IP to SoC team.

In this unit, you will study about the possible interfaces of Image Signal Processing IP and main blocks of UVM based IP Level Verification Environment. Next in this unit, UVM test bench architecture is described. Procedure to do synchronization between Register sequences and data sequences is also described. Finally, flow of IP level Verification Environment is described.

Objectives

After studying this unit, you will be able to:

- understand the importance of IP level verification

- understand the basic blocks of System Verilog UVM based IP level verification environment

- define the collective components of UVM test bench architecture

- understand the top environment class of IP level verification environment

2.2 Basic blocks of SV-UVM based IP Level Verification Environment

In our case of an image signal processing IP, there are *A* input video data interfaces, *C* output video data interfaces, *B* memory interfaces, *D* output Interrupts and *E* register interfaces, where *A, B, C, D* and *E* values can be from 0 to any arbitrary number.

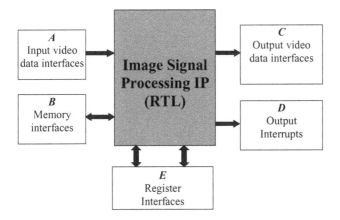

Figure 2-1: Image Signal Processing IP Block Diagram

For verifying these interfaces, dedicated UVCs are used. In case of register interface(s), register interface UVC and UVM_REG register model are used. Similarly for video data interface(s), video data interface UVC is used and for verification of interrupts, generic interrupt checker is used.

Note that there can be multiple instances of these UVC's in a verification environment. Each agent is configured separately and any combination of agent configurations can coexist in the same environment.

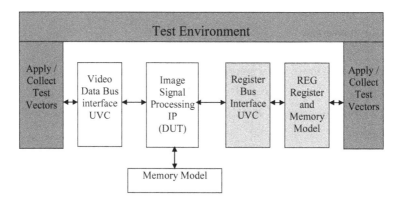

Figure 2-2: Basic blocks of System Verilog UVM based IP Level Verification Environment

Therefore in above case, *E* instances of register interface UVC agents, M (M = max (A, C)) instances of video data interface UVC agents and D instances of interrupt checker are used to interface with a DUT. Figure 2.2 illustrates the basic blocks of System Verilog UVM based IP Level Verification Environment.

Self-Assessment Questions:

1. Why is IP level verification so important?

2. What is need of an UVC?

3. To verify the register interface of an IP, _____ is used.

2.3 UVM Testbench Architecture

The Architecture of UVM testbench is modular to ease the reuse of collective verification components either at a higher level of integration in the same project (vertical reuse) or in different projects (horizontal reuse). There are two main component types which are used to enable reuse - the agent and the env.

2.3.1 The Agent

Most of the DUTs have a number of different signal interfaces, each of which has their own protocol. The UVM agent assembles together a group of uvm_components focused around a specific pin-level interface. The objective of the agent is to give a verification component which allows users to generate and monitor pin level transactions. A System Verilog package is used to collect all the classes joined with an agent together into one namespace.

The contents of an agent package include:

   a) *A Sequence_item* -The agent will have one or more sequence items which are used to either define what pin level activity will be generated by the agent or to report on what pin level activity has been observed by the agent.

   b) *A Driver* - The driver is responsible for converting the data inside a series of sequence_items into signal level transactions.

   c) *A Sequencer* - The function of the sequencer is to transfer sequence_items from a sequence where they are generated to/from a driver.

   d) *A Monitor* - The monitor observes port level activity and converts its observations into sequence_items which are sent to components such as scoreboards which use them to analyse what is happening in the testbench.

   e) *Configuration object* - A container object, used to pass information to the agent which affects what it does and how it is built and connected.

2.3.2 The Env

In UVM, The environment, or env class, is a container component where sub-components orientated around a block, or around a collection of blocks are grouped together at higher levels of integration.

In UVM testbench, the environment (env) is used to assemble together the agents needed to communicate with the DUT's interfaces in one place. Similar to the agent, the different classes associated with the env are organized into a System Verilog package, which imports the agent packages. In addition to the agents, the env contains some or all of the following types of components:

a) ***Configuration object*** - The env have a configuration object using which the test case developer is able to control which of the environments sub-components are built. The env configuration object contains a handle for the configuration object for each of the agents that it contains.

b) ***Scoreboards*** - A scoreboard is an analysis component that checks whether the DUT is behaving correctly or not. UVM scoreboards use analysis transactions from the monitors implemented inside agents. A scoreboard usually compare transactions from at least two agents, therefore, it is generally present in the env.

c) ***Predictors*** - A predictor is a component that calculates the response expected from the stimulus, it is used with other components such as the scoreboard.

d) ***Virtual Sequencers*** - A virtual sequencer is used in the stimulus generation process to allow a single sequence to control stimulus generation activity via several agents

e) ***Functional Coverage Monitors*** - A functional coverage monitor class contains one or more cover groups which are used to collect functional coverage information related to what has happened in a testbench during a test case. A functional coverage monitor is generally specific to a DUT.

Figure 2.3 illustrates the different Components of Universal Verification Component (UVC).

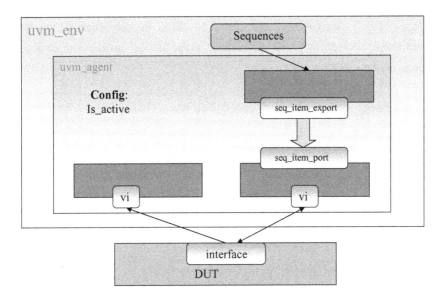

Figure 2-3: Different Components of Universal Verification Component (UVC)

Self-Assessment Questions:

4. Name two components of UVM testbench architecture that enables reuse?

5. What is the purpose of agent? Give difference between active and passive agent.

6. List the types of components that environment has in IP level UVM testbench.

2.4 Top environment class

Figure 2.4 shows the Imaging IP level verification environment's top environment class. Scoreboard of Imaging IP level verification environment need information both from control bus UVC and data bus UVC. Thus, scoreboard class is instantiated inside IP level verification environment's top environment class. Environment classes of both data bus UVC and control bus UVC are also instantiated inside verification environment's top environment class. IP top environment class is instantiated inside 'Testcase' class.

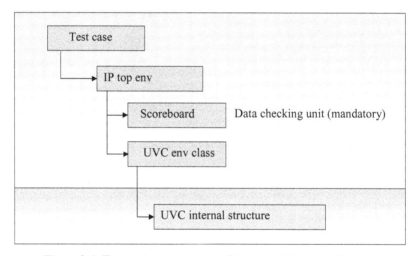

Figure 2-4: Top environment class of Imaging IP level verification environment.

The synchronization between the sequences of data bus UVC and control bus UVC is explained from the below diagram.

Register sequencer executes register operation sequences according to the register model specification & configuration. Similarly, Data Bus sequencer also executes data operation sequences according to the data bus specification & configuration.

Virtual Sequencer Controls timing and data flow of entire system via reusable sequences.

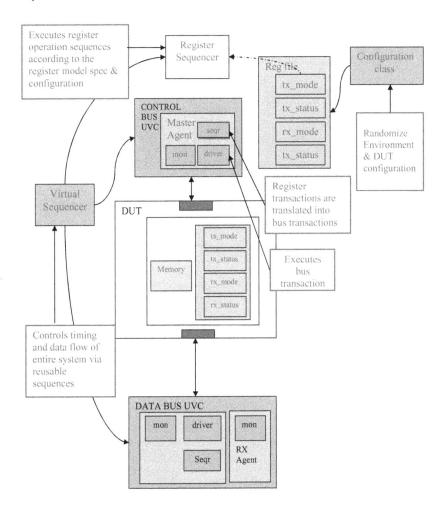

Figure 2-5: Synchronization between register sequences and data sequences

Since register or data sequences, sequencers and drivers are focused on point interfaces, IP level verification environment have a virtual sequence to co-ordinate the stimulus across register and data interfaces and the interactions between them. Virtual sequence controls the register and data sequences.

A virtual sequence runs on a virtual sequencer by adding code that gets the handles to the sub-sequencers (register sequencer and data sequencer) from the virtual sequencer. Virtual sequences are extended from a base class that does the sequencer handle assignment. The virtual sequencer's sub-sequencer references is assigned during the connect phase.

Virtual sequencer is inserted inside the environment of IP level testbench, with the connect method of the environment is used to assign the sub-sequencer handles of Register sequencer and data bus UVC sequencer. Since the virtual sequence is in overall control of the simulation, it is created in the test run method and is started on the virtual sequencer - i.e. virtual_sequence.start (virtual_sequencer);

Detailed information on Register model is given in chapter 6.

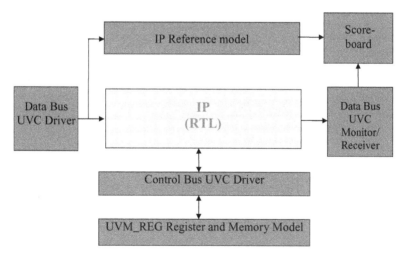

Figure 2-6: IP Level Verification Environment

In IP level verification environment for an imaging IP as shown in figure 2.6, UVM_REG register and memory model is used to model registers and memories of DUT. DUT registers are written/read via control bus UVC. RTL control bus interface acts as target and control bus UVC acts as initiator. The target control interface of the IP is driven by control bus UVC (configured as initiator).After register programming is done, image data(random/user-defined) is driven to the data bus interface by the data bus UVC and the same data is also driven to the reference model.

Output of the IP is received by the receiver/monitor of the data bus UVC. Scoreboard compares the output of RTL and reference model and gives the status saying whether the both output matches or not.

Detailed information on Scoreboard is given in chapter 7.

Self-Assessment Questions:

7. Is scoreboard important? Justify your answer.

8. What does virtual sequencer do?

9. Explain how DUT register gets configured?

3. Universal Verification Methodology based Reusable Subsystem Level Verification Environment

Structure

3.1 Introduction

At subsystem level, various IPs are connected may be via Interconnects and becomes more complex from verification perspective. It is very important to reuse the IP level verification environment to reduce the verification effort at Subsystem level.

In this unit you will study about the universal verification methodology based reusable subsystem level verification environment. Next in this unit, you will be acquainted with the importance of reuse of environment and sequences.

Objectives

After studying this unit, you will be able to:

- assess the importance of reuse of IP level verification environment at subsystem level
- understand the reuse of IP level verification environment
- understand the reuse of sequences

3.2 Reuse of Environment

When IPs are integrated to create a sub-system, vertical reuse can be achieved by reusing the environments used in each of the IP level test benches merged together into a higher level environment. The IP level environments provide all of the structures required testing each IP, but as a result of the integration process, not all the IP level interfaces are exposed at the boundary and so some of the functionality of the IP level environments will be redundant. The integration level environment then needs to be configured to make agents connected to internal interfaces passive, or possibly even not to include an agent at all. This configuration is done in the test, and the configuration object for each sub-environment is nested inside the configuration object for the environment at the next level of hierarchy. Thus, all internal IP level verification environments are configured as Passive agents whereas Interface IP level verification environments are used as Active agents. UVM-ML (Multiple Language) approach helps us in reusing the existing verification components.

Self-Assessment Questions:

1. Give reasons why reuse of IP level verification environment so important?

2. When Integration level environment needs to be configured, all internal IP level verification environments are configured as _____ and Interface IP level verification environments are used as _____.

3.3 Reuse of Sequences

Register read/write sequences: UVM_REG register read/write sequences read and write address mapped registers in the DUT. As UVM_REG have API that is independent of the bus protocol and hence can be reused at Subsystem and SoC level as at Subsystem and SoC level base address of these registers changes and in register sequences, registers can be accessed using name or type also. UVM_REG register package is used to lookup the register address by name. UVM_REG register package built-in sequences supports this kind of abstraction. This makes these sequences reusable and maintainable because there is no need to update the sequence each time a register address changes.

Virtual sequences on accessible interfaces (IP3, IP4, IP5 and IP6) at subsystem-level: These sequences are reusable from IP level to subsystem-level; some of them can be used to verify the integration of IP's into sub-system.

When creating integrated verification environments that reuse IP level verification environments, the virtual sequencers at the different levels of the testbench hierarchy can be chained together, allowing virtual sequences or sub-sequences to be run at any level. To achieve this level of flexibility, both the sub-sequencer handles and the virtual sequencer handles are encapsulated at each successive level.

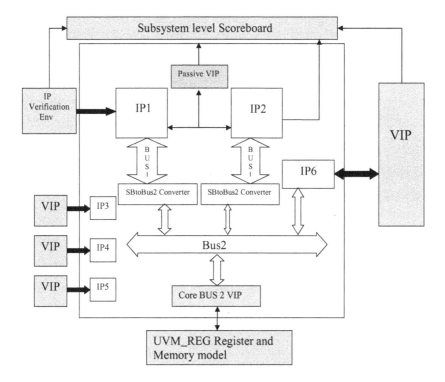

Figure 3-1: Reuse of IP Level Verification Environment at Sub-System Level

Self-Assessment Questions:

3. Why we use UVM_REG register package?

4. How can we reuse the sequences?

4. Universal Verification Methodology based SoC Level Verification Environment

Structure

4.1 Introduction

    4.1.1 Objectives

4.2 Reuse of Sub-System Level Verification Environment at SoC Level

4.3 Incisive Software Extension (ISX) Approach

4.4 Virtual Register Interface (VRI) Approach

4.1 Introduction

Various subsystems are integrated together to build a SoC and make a verification task very challenging at SoC level. There are various challenges at SoC level verification like –

a. How to reuse subsystem level verification environment at SoC level to minimize the verification effort at SoC level

b. Connectivity between IPs

c. Verification of System Level scenarios

d. How to synchronize "C" testcases running on Core with IP/Subsystem level verification environments to enable maximum reuse

At IP/Subsystem level verification, Cores are usually stub to do verification and BUS UVCs are used to generate BUS traffic which can be replaced by Core at SoC level. Working with a verification component at the SoC level makes it difficult to create activity that will be similar to the way the design will behave with CPU and software. An even more important challenge is what to do about SoC initialization?

    UVM based Verification Environment – Theory and Practice

Sometimes, there are thousands of programmable registers that must be configured before SoC is ready to do any meaningful activity. Besides being a tedious process, the motivation for writing a long initialization sequence just for verification is low because in the end it's the job of the software to initialize the SoC, not the verification engineer. The result is duplication of effort.

In this unit, you will study about the universal verification methodology based SoC level verification environment. Then, two main approaches (ISX and VRI) are described to reuse the IP/Subsystem level verification environment when we replace Host BFM with actual Core.

Objectives

After studying this unit, you will be able to:

- understand the major challenges faced for verification at SoC level
- assess the importance of reuse of IP/Subsystem level verification environment at SoC level
- understand the various approaches for reuse of IP/Subsystem level verification environment at SoC level

4.2 Reuse of Sub-System Level Verification Environment at SoC Level

At SoC level, we reuse register sequences and all internal IP/Subsystem level verification environments are configured as Passive agents whereas Interface IP level verification environments are used as Active agents. Since the register sequences are independent of BUS protocol, it enables to reuse the register sequences with different BUS at IP/Subsystem/SoC level.

When we replace Host BFM with actual Core then it becomes challenging to reuse the existing verification environment as with Core in place, "C" testcases are used to do verification. At SoC level, it is important to verify the hardware and software works seamlessly together to deliver the functionality and performance of the system. Below are the 2 approaches –

1) Use of incisive software Extension (ISX) to reuse the IP/Subsystem level verification environment.
2) To reuse IP/Subsystem verification environments from "C" testcases running on the Core.

Self-Assessment Questions:

1. What are the major challenges for verification at SoC level?

4.3 Incisive Software Extension (ISX) Approach

Incisive Software Extension (ISX) is used to reuse the IP/Subsystem level verification environment. In this approach, Hardware/Software Co-Verification technique is used in which "C" routines are controlled/called from HVLs like "e" or "System Verilog". It enables to do constrained random and coverage driven verification of embedded software. It enables users to provide –

a. Constrained random values to "C" functions parameters
b. Functional coverage of "C" variables
c. Random calling of "C" functions

This helps in performing thorough verification of hardware and software together and enables in getting corner cases.

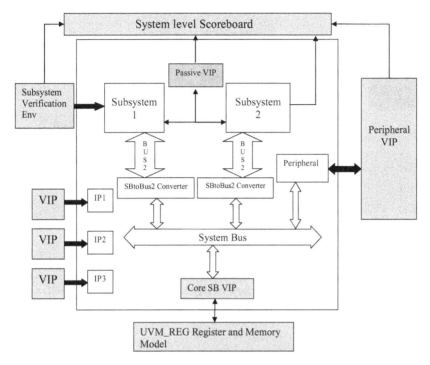

Figure 4-1: Reuse of Sub-System Level Verification Environment at SoC Level

Virtual sequences from IP/Subsystem level verification environment are reused at SoC level. In this approach, "C" test cases are controlled from virtual sequences. A SW UVC is created which enabled control of "C" test cases from HVL verification environments. Since the SW UVC is in HVL, it can be used with rest of the SoC level verification environment which enables reuse of the IP/Subsystem level verification environment. At IP/Subsystem level, virtual sequences are calling register sequences over HOST BFM, which can be reused to call "C" routines which is performing register read/write to IPs via SW UVCs. SW UVC contains sequences which correspond to each "C" routine which is executing on the core. From Virtual sequences we can call these SW UVC sequences which in turn will call "C" routines.

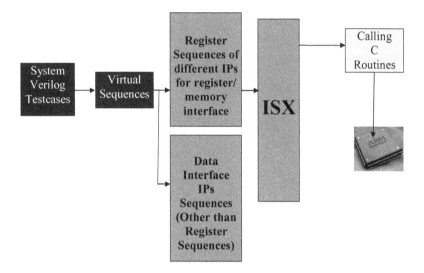

Figure 4-2: Use of ISX (Incisive Software Extensions) in UVM based SoC Level Verification Environment

In this approach, by connecting and controlling the C functions from the verification environments, the best of both worlds is achieved which is running C code on the CPU and the generation, checking and coverage provided by Coverage Driven Verification environment.

Incisive Software Extension is using the concept of Generic Software Adapter (GSA) which is used to connect to and control embedded software. It enables verification engineers to hook their IP/Subsystem level verification environments at SoC level executing embedded software.

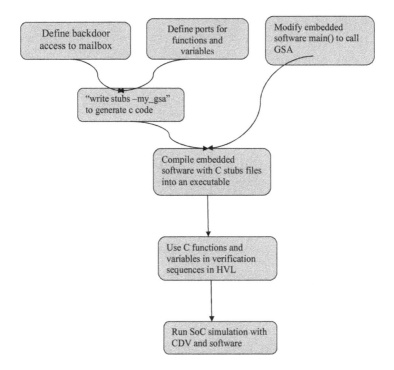

Figure 4-3: GSA Integration Flow. Source: Chip Design Magazine.

Specman contains ways to connect verification environments written in e language to designs under verification (DUV) written in VHDL, Verilog, and SystemC. GSA connects the e environment to embedded software. Now the verification environment can control both the hardware design and the software running on the CPU. GSA works in any co-simulation environment using any type of CPU model.

"e" ports are used to connect C functions and variables to the verification environment. The e language has different types of ports available to communicate with the DUV (the embedded software in this case). GSA uses simple and event ports to read and write variables in the C code and method ports to call C functions.

Unique ability of Specman to "generate stubs" is the key to GSA. Using different languages for the verification and the design may seem like drawback to some, especially when only 1 DUV (an HDL design) is being verified but when the DUV is both hardware and embedded software this separation of verification language from DUV and the ability to connect to multiple, different types of DUVs at the same time is a great advantage. The stub generation process makes the connection between the verification environment and the embedded software completely automated. The overall procedure to perform CDV with embedded software is shown in Figure 4.3.

Self-Assessment Questions:

2. What are the benefits of using ISX?

4.4 Virtual Register Interface (VRI) Approach

Second approach is to reuse IP/Subsystem verification environments from "C" testcases running on the Core. Today, most of the embedded test infrastructure uses some adhoc mechanism like "shared memory" or synchronization mechanism for controlling simple Bus functional models (BFMs) from embedded software.

In order to provide full controllability to the "C" test developer over these verification components, a virtual register interface layer is created over these verification environments which provides the access to the sequences of these verification environment to the embedded software enabling configuration and control of these verification environments and provide the same exhaustive verification at SoC Level.

This approach addresses the following aspects of verification at SoC Level:

- Configuration and control of verification components from embedded software
- Reusability of verification environments from IP to SoC
- Enables reusability of testcases from IP to SoC
- Providing integration testcases to SoC team which is developed by IP verification teams.

It has been achieved by using Virtual Register Interface (VRI) layer over Verification components. VRI layer over verification components is -

- A virtual layer over verification environment to make it controllable from embedded software
- Provides high level C APIs hiding low level implementation

Main advantage of VRI is Verification IP (VIP) and Test Code Reuse. The same VIP and Test code can be reused from IP-level to SoC level verification.

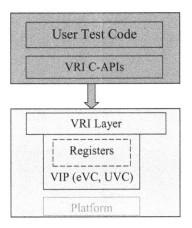

Figure 4-4: Virtual Register Interface (VRI)

Figure 4-5 shows SoC level Functional Verification Environment where using virtual sequences, SoC DUT is simultaneously bombarded at all Interfaces in an automated and coordinated way. Virtual sequence is controlling the stimulus generation using several sequencers of HOST Bus UVC, USB UVC, and Ethernet UVC etc.

Here programming of SoC Registers is done using Control/Host Bus UVC and not from the actual Core. All testcases are in System Verilog.

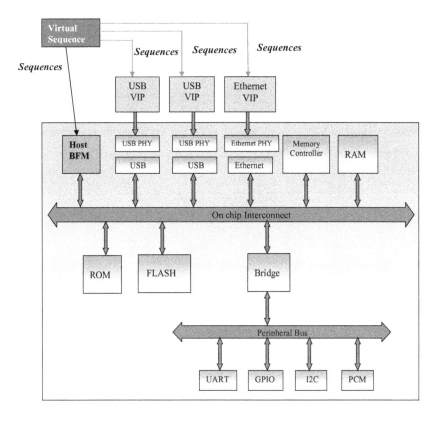

Figure 4-5: SoC level Functional Verification Environment using UVM

UVM based Verification Environment – Theory and Practice

Figure 4-6 shows SoC level Functional Verification Environment where Test SW mixed with Host BFM. VRI APIs are converted to Host Bus UVC's transactions. Concept of Virtual Register Interface (VRI) is described as below.

The basic interface between embedded processors and internal IPs (e.g., peripheral devices) in a SoC is a set of control and status registers. These registers that are usually located in the memory space of the system (memory mapped) are part of the IP Implementation and they represent features of the IP itself. Similarly, any external verification IP (VIP) like Ethernet VIP used for the verification of a SoC could be interfaced to an embedded processor through a set of control and status registers in the same way we do with hardware IPs.

Virtual Register Interface (or VRI) exposes the functionality of the VIPs (e.g., VIP configuration or VIP sequences) in the form of a register map suitable to be controlled by an embedded processor. The VRI is composed of a frontend (FE) component, specific of the physical interface where it is connected, a bridge component to converts TLM packets generated by the front-end into internal VRI packets and a set of VRI back-end components (VRI-BE) each one devoted to interface a specific VIP or to provide dedicated randomization capabilities. In the UVM terminology the VRI front-end is a monitor and is typically connected at SoC-level to the ports of an embedded static RAM. The bridge converts a FE-specific memory packet generated by the FE and carrying an address, a data value, and a direction into a VRI-specific memory packet propagating the same information. Each memory transaction flowing through the interface where the VRI is connected is captured and forwarded to all the internal VRI-BE components. Each of them can be programmed to be sensitive to a particular memory address and, in case of matching against the memory address of the incoming memory packet; the data value is used as a selector to trigger different actions the VRI BE component can execute.

Figure 4-7 shows SoC level Functional Verification Environment where Test SW mixed with bare metal SW. DUT Processor acts like virtual sequencer. Core is executing the C test cases along with VRI API.

Figure 4-8 shows VRI layer over UVC used for IP verification and Figure 4-9 shows Reusing the IP level verification environment at SoC Level using VRI layer.

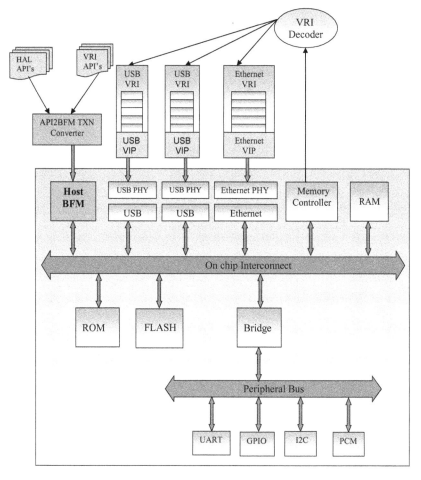

Figure 4-6: Test SW mixed with Host BFM

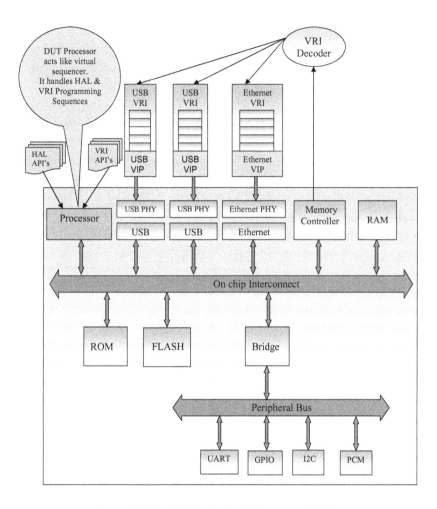

Figure 4-7: Test SW mixed with bare metal SW

An example of C test case using VRI interface is as follows –

```
vr_enet_packet pkt;
vr_enet_packet rx_pkt;
rx_pkt.data = new vri_uint8_t[2000]; //create buffer for receiving data

pkt.packet_kind = ETHERNET_802_3;
pkt.data_length = 0; //RANDOM DATA
pkt.dest_addr_high = 0x11ff;
pkt.src_addr_high = 0x2288;
pkt.tag_kind = UNTAGGED;
pkt.tag_prefix = 0x1234;
pkt.s_vlan_tag_prefix = 0x5678;
pkt.err_code = 0;
for (int i=0;i<100;i++) {
  pkt.dest_addr_low = i;
  pkt.src_addr_low = i+1;
  enet_send_pkt(0,&pkt);     //send packet to ENET UVC instance0 (MAC)
  enet_recv_pkt(1,&rx_pkt); //receive packet from ENET UVC instance1 (PHY)
  compare_pkt(pkt,rx_pkt);
};
```

Some important points regarding VRI layer are as follows:

1. Using VRI layer, Verification Environment users can write C test cases to control the System Verilog/e VIP's. It gives flexibility to Verification Environment users to use the VIP's without knowing SV/e.

2. Writing C test cases to control System Verilog/e VIP's doesn't mean that we can write only directed test cases. Through VRI layer, we can do SW data randomization also.

3. Verification Environment users can write both C and System Verilog test cases to control the same VIP.

4. VRI layer gives Verification Environment users flexibility to use same test cases at IP/SoC level functional Verification as well as for Validation.

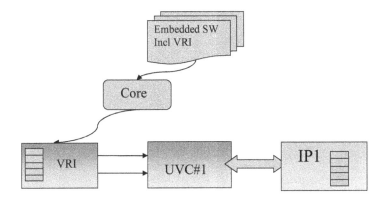

Figure 4-8: VRI layer over UVC used for IP verification

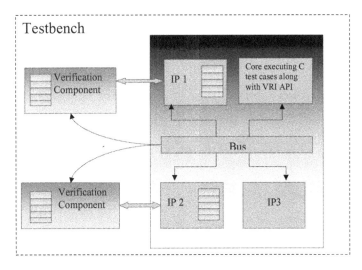

Figure 4-9: Reusing the IP level Verification Environment at SoC Level (using VRI layer)

Self-Assessment Questions:

3. Explain VRI layer for IP verification.

4. List advantages of VRI.

5. IPXACT Flow

Structure

5.1 Introduction

    5.1.1 Objectives

5.2 IP-XACT Flow

5.1 Introduction

SPIRIT symbolizes *"Structure for Packaging, Integrating and Re-using IP within Tool-flows"*. It is a Standard based on XML open format and it describes:

- Register Map
- Bus Interfaces
- Top-level I/O
- Others including interconnect, constraints …

IPXACT is developed by The SPIRIT Consortium (http://spiritconsortium.org).It is originally developed for delivering IP descriptions of components to EDA tools, and for exchanging design's IP descriptions between EDA tools. Now it is starting to be used in other areas, including the description of debugger targets. A design or component's IPXACT description composed of a set of XML documents referring to one another. Main XML document types are:

1. Design – A high level design description.
2. Component – A component type description, including interfaces, registers and memory maps
3. Bus Definition – A bus type description.
4. References between IP-XACT document are by 4 element identifier (vendor, library, name and version; often abbreviated to VLNV).

---

5. IP-XACT also defines an interface for generators (parsers), which are utilities invoked from Design Environments to process IP-XACT data.

In this unit, you will understand IPXACT flow in detail. Next in this unit, applications of IP-XACT tools to automatically generate UVM Verification Environment files are described.

Objectives

After studying this unit, you will be able to:

- understand the IP-XACT Flow

- understand the applications of IP-XACT tools to automatically generate UVM Verification Environment files

5.2 IP-XACT Flow

In System Verilog UVM based Verification Environment as described in earlier units, register description file for register model, address map file, sequences file, functional Coverage file, data checker file to compare the output of RTL with output of Python Reference model are IP/SoC specific which need to be modified for every IP/SoC. Therefore, IP-XACT based tools are used for generation of these files. First, the register map description has to be provided in XML-based IP-XACT view.

XML-based IP-XACT view is automatically generated from the Register Specification Document using spec2spirit (Specification to SPIRIT) script.

In Data checker file, there is invocation of Python model containing attributes thus; automatic generation of data checker file requires the mapping between the registers/register-fields/parameters of RTL and the attributes of Python model.

In spirit2uvm (SPIRIT to UVM Environment files) script, there is one input file

— IP-XACT view of register map, containing the register description.

spirit2uvm IP-XACT based tool generates IP/SoC specific files which are used in the System Verilog UVM based verification environment as shown in figure 5-1.

Map file for mapping between the registers/register-fields/parameters of RTL and the attributes of Python model is also generated from IP-XACT based tool.

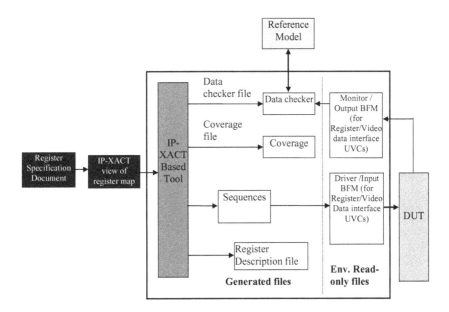

Figure 5-1: Usage of IP-XACT Flow in Universal Verification Methodology based Verification Environment

Various spirit scripts used for automatically generation of UVM based Verification Environment files are as follows:

a. spec2regbank (Specification to Register bank files and SPIRIT file)
b. spec2spirit (Specification to SPIRIT)
c. spirit2uvm (SPIRIT to UVM Environment files)
d. spec2uvm (Specification to UVM Environment files)
e. spec2spec (Specification to Specification)

These scripts are described in detail below.

5.2.1 spec2regbank (Specification to Register bank files and SPIRIT file)

The main function of the spec2regbank script is to generate the Xml files, RTL Register bank files and user defined files (udf) of the particular IP .These files are generated from the Register Specification file (mif/docx) of that particular IP. Register Specification file should be created following some guidelines/templates so that spec2regbank can parse the required information (registers/register fields/reset values etc.) from it. Generated Register bank files are used in RTL design of that IP and Generated xml file is used by spirit2uvm script to generate System Verilog UVM Verification Environment files which are IP/SoC dependent.

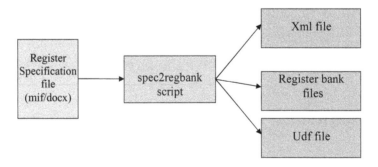

Figure 5-2: spec2regbank script

spec2regbank script is wrapper script over spec2spirit and spirit2regbank (SPIRIT to Register Bank) scripts.

Self-Assessment Questions:

1. Name the input file for spec2regbank script.

5.2.2 spirit2uvm (SPIRIT to UVM Environment files)

The xml file generated from spec2spirit script is used as input file for running spirit2uvm script and the generated output files are UVM based Verification Environment files like Register description file, Functional Coverage file, Sequences file, reference model task file for generating execution script for python reference model, address map file etc.

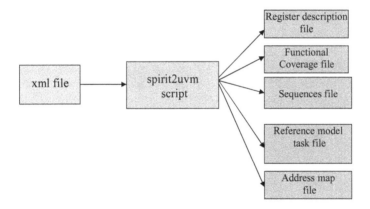

Figure 5-3: spirit2uvm script

In other words, 'spirit2uvm' generator is a command line utility which takes in a SPIRIT component and generates the following outputs from a SPIRIT description of a component memory/register.

- <ip>_uvm_reg_def.sv

- <ip>_seq.sv

- <ip>_addr_map.sv

- <ip>_*_invalid_addr.sv

- <ip>_reference_model_tasks.sv

- <ip>_reg_seq.sv

- <ip>_*_func_cov.sv

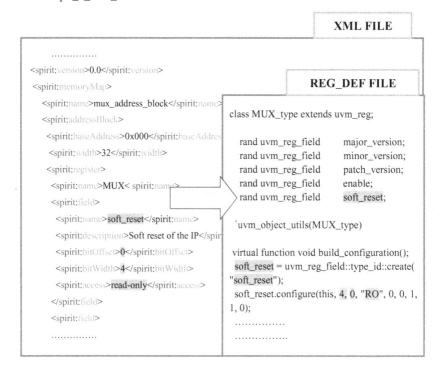

Figure 5-4: XML to REG_DEF file conversion

The figure 5-4 shows sample example of input xml file and generated output register definition (reg_def) file. The xml file provides all the basic information of the IP such as IP's base address (<spirit:baseAddress>0x000</spirit:baseAddress>), register's name (<spirit:name>MUX<spirit:name>), register field bit width (<spirit:bitWidth>4</ spirit:bitWidth>), register field bit offset (<spirit:bitOffset >0</spirit:bitOffset>), register field accessibility (<spirit:access>read-only< /spirit:access>) etc. From the given information in input xml file, corresponding register definition (reg_def) file is generated using spirit2uvm script.

5.2.3 spec2uvm (Specification to UVM Environment files)

spec2uvm script is wrapper script over spec2regbank and spirit2uvm scripts and is used to convert register specification file into RTL register bank files and System Verilog UVM based Verification Environment files like register description file, functional coverage file, sequences file, reference model task file for generating execution script for python reference model, address map file etc.

Self-Assessment Questions:

2. What does spirit script do?

3. IPXACT based tools are used for generation of Verification Environment files. Name them.

4. What is the use of Data checker file?

5. Name input file for IPXACT based tool.

6. Name the input and output files for spirit2uvm script.

5.2.4 spec2spec (Specification to Specification)

Various IPs are connected together to build a subsystem and various subsystems are integrated together to build a SoC. Thus, at SoC level, there is large number of IP's connected together. For each IP, register specification file in mif/docx format is written. Using spec2spirit script, xml file of the particular IP is generated and using spirit2uvm script, System Verilog UVM based Verification Environment files are generated.

Specification files of all IP's are merged together using spec2spec (Specification to Specification) script to generate XML description of the SoC level register/memory specification.

There is one input mif/docx file to spec2spec script to give following information –
1. Location of xml files of each IP.
2. Offset address information of each IP at SoC level and
3. Prefix to be added in registers names of each IP at SoC level.

spirit2uvm script uses generated SoC/Top level xml file and generates System Verilog UVM based verification environment files at SoC level.

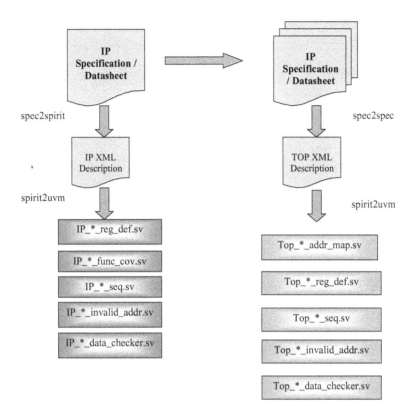

Figure 5-5: IP-XACT Flow for generating IP and SoC level Verification Environment files

There are two ways to develop SoC level verification environment files –

- Reuse already generated and tested IP level verification environment files.
- Generate SoC level Verification Environment files using spirit2uvm script.

Self-Assessment Questions:

7. Name the input and output files for spec2spec script.

6. Register and Memory Verification

Structure

6.1 Introduction

    6.1.1 Objectives

6.2 Register model

6.3 Built-in Register Tests

6.4 Data flow

6.1 Introduction

The UVM_REG register and memory model gives a path for tracking the register content of a DUT and a suitable layer for accessing register and memory areas within the DUT.

The register model abstraction shows an image of the structure of a hardware-software register specification. As register specification is the common reference specification for hardware design and verification engineers and is also used by software engineers for developing firmware layer software. It is paramount that all three groups refer a common specification and it is very important that the design is verified against an accurate model.

In this unit you will study about the basics of register and memory model. Also usage of UVM_REG register and memory model for programming of registers and memories of Sensor and Co-Processor designs is described in detail. Next in this unit, UVM_REG register test cases are described.

Objectives

After studying this unit, you will be able to:

- understand the register model

- understand the UVM_REG register test cases

6.2 Register Model

The UVM register model is designed to ease efficient verification of programmable hardware. When used effectively, UVM register model raises the level of stimulus abstraction and makes reuse of the resultant stimulus code straight-forward, either when the DUT block is reused as a sub-component or when there is a change in the DUT register address map.

Main purpose of the UVM_REG register model is to make it easier to write reusable register/memory sequences that access hardware registers and memory areas. The register model data structure is designed to show an image of the DUT hierarchy and this makes it easier to write reusable and abstract stimulus in terms of hardware blocks, registers and fields, memories rather than working at a lower bit pattern level of abstraction. The register model contains a number of read/write access methods which sequences use to read and write registers. These methods results in conversion of generic register transactions into the target bus transactions.

The UVM register package contains built-in test sequences library which is used to perform most of the basic register and memory tests, such as testing of register reset values and testing of the register and memory data paths. Using register attributes, these tests can be disabled for those locations of the register or memory map where they are not relevant.

When a programmable DUT has its registers set up to support a particular mode of operation, then stimulus is referred to as configuration. The register model supports auto-configuration, a course of action whereby the contents of the register model are forced into a state that represents a device configuration using constrained randomization and then transferred into the DUT.

The model supports both front door and back door access to the DUT registers. Front door access uses the control bus agent in the test bench and register accesses use the normal control bus transfer protocol. Back door access bypass the normal bus interface logic and uses simulator data base access routines to directly force or observe the register hardware bits in zero simulation time.

As a verification environment gradually develops, verification users need to develop analysis components such as scoreboards and functional coverage monitors which refers to the contents of the register model in order to check behaviour of the DUT or to make sure that it has been tested in all required configurations.

In Imaging Verification Environment, UVM_REG Register and Memory model is used for efficient verification of register and memory. It contains built-in mechanisms with predefined types for efficient modeling. This is used in conjunction with the register/control interface UVC, so that whenever the IP/SoC registers are read/written, the associated UVM_REG Register and Memory model pre-defined registers are also updated and IP/SoC register contents are verified by a self-checking mechanism.

The UVM_REG Register and Memory model addresses following aspects of memory and registers:
- Address management
- Register modeling

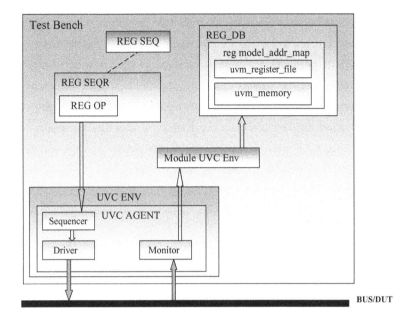

Figure 6-1: Register and Memory package Architecture

Register and memory package have the following components in addition to the basic Verification Environment elements (env, agents etc.):

- Register File — Represents DUT agent registers. It contains a list of consecutive registers.
- Address Map — Represents the address space. It maps the register files and the memory blocks (if any) in the address space, and it contains references to them. In a very simple environment with only one register file, an address map may seem redundant. Address maps gain importance in environments with multiple register files.

- The Register Sequencer and Sequences - The uvm_reg package uses the familiar UVM sequence mechanism to randomize and drive register and memory sequences. In a sequence, we can randomly select a register object from the REG_DB, randomize it, set the access direction (read or write), and perform the operation. Register/memory operation sequences look much like any other UVM sequence. Using the sequence mechanism allows us to create reusable sequences to support different configuration modes, use an existing sequence as a sub-sequence, traverse through all the register in the addresses range, and much more. An API is provided to perform read and write operations.

Self-Assessment Questions:

1. What is the use of register model?

2. Does register model supports front door and back door access to the DUT registers? Justify your answer.

6.3 Built-In Register Tests

Built-in register test cases allow user to execute pre-defined register test-cases. The uvm_reg package has built-in sequence library.

The basic built-in sequences are as follow:

1. **uvm_reg_hw_reset_seq:** This is used to test the hard reset value of the register. Here it first resets the DUT and then, reads all the register in the block via all the available address map and check their value with the specified reset value. If "NO_REG_TEST" or "NO_REG_HW_RESET_TEST" bit type resource is specified in "REG::" namespace then that block or register is not tested.

2. **uvm_reg_single_bit_bash:** This is used to verify the implementation of single register by writing 1's or 0's to all the bits via address map, checking whether it is correctly set or cleared, based on field access policy specified for field containing the target bit. If "NO_REG_TEST" or "NO_REG_BIT_BASH_ TEST" bit type resource is specified in "REG::" namespace then that register is not tested.

3. **uvm_reg_bit_bash:** This test verifies the implementation of every register in the block by executing uvm_reg_single_bit_bash sequence on it. If "NO_REG_TEST" or "NO_REG_BIT_BASH_TEST" bit type resource is specified in "REG::" namespace then that block or register is not tested.

4. **uvm_reg_single_access_seq:** This test is used to verify the accessibility of the register. First it writes to register then reads the value via back-door so as to confirm that the value was written correctly. And similarly it writes through backdoor and then read the value of the register via address map so as to confirm the accessibility of the register. If "NO_REG_TEST" or "NO_REG_ACCESS_TEST" bit type resource is specified in "REG::" namespace then that register is not tested. Also those register with no back-door or those with read-only field or with unknown access policies cannot be tested.

5. **uvm_reg_access_seq:** This test is used to verify the accessibility of all the register in a block by executing uvm_reg_access_seq on all register. If "NO_REG_TEST" or "NO_REG_ACCESS_TEST" bit type resource is specified in "REG::" namespace then that block or register is not tested.

6. **uvm_reg_mem_access_seq:** This is used to verify the accessibility of the register and that of memories in a block by executing uvm_reg_access_seq and uvm_reg_mem_access_seq respectively on register and memories within it. . If "NO_REG_TEST" or "NO_REG_ACCESS_TEST" bit type resource is specified in "REG::" namespace then that block or register is not tested.

7. **uvm_reg_shared_access_seq:** This is used to verify the accessibility of the shared register. Shared register are those which are shared between two or more physical interface which means that they are associated with more than one uvm_reg_map instance. The test actually verifies the accessibility of the register by writing to it through one address map and then confirming it by read the value via another address map. If "NO_REG_TEST" or "NO_REG_SHARED_ACCESS_TEST" bit type resource is specified in "REG::" namespace then that block or register is not tested.

8. **uvm_mem_shared_access_seq:** This is used to verify the accessibility of the shared memory by writing through each address map and reading them through other address map in which memory is readable. If "NO_REG_TEST" or "NO_REG_SHARED_ACCESS_TEST" or "NO_MEM_SHARED_ACCESS _TEST" bit type resource is specified in "REG::" namespace then that memory is not tested.

An example of using **uvm_reg_hw_reset_seq** is described below:

```
class hw_reset_seq_test extends register_test;
   uvm_component_utils(hw_reset_seq_test)
   uvm_reg_hw_reset_seq mTestSeq;

   function new(string name = "hw_reset_seq_test", uvm_component parent);
      super.new(name,parent);
      set_config_string("*.reg_sequencer","default_sequence",
"uvm_reg_hw_reset_seq" );
   endfunction // new

   function automatic void build_phase(uvm_phase phase);
      super.build_phase(phase);
   endfunction
   extern task run_phase ( uvm_phase phase);
endclass

task hw_reset_seq_test::run_phase ( uvm_phase phase );
   phase.raise_objection ( this );
   super.run_phase ( phase );
   mTestSeq = uvm_reg_hw_reset_seq::type_id::create ( "mTestSeq", this );
   mTestSeq.model = mysve.regmodel;
   mTestSeq.start (mysve.reg_sequencer);
   phase.drop_objection(this);
endtask : run_phase
```

Self-Assessment Questions:

3. List some of the built-in register test cases.

4. Name the attribute for which register and memory will be disabled for testing.

5. _____ package has built-in sequences.

6.4 Data Flow

In test case file, register_test (derived class of uvm_class) set the default sequence (e.g. hard reset sequence). Hard reset sequence is a built-in sequence which applies for all selected registers inside container (register database). register_test have the instance of top level environment class (uvm_env).

Top level environment class (uvm_env) has the instances of register UVC environment class, register database and register sequencer. Register database holds address maps. Address map captures register files of multiple blocks. Address map holds register attributes and expected values. Register sequencer executes register operation sequences according to the register model specification and configuration.

The UVM_REG sequencer is layered on top of register/control UVC master sequencer. The control bus UVC master emulates the CPU as it programs, controls, and supervises other devices on the bus. Every read and write operation is translated to protocol-specific control bus transactions. This isolation between register operation and control bus transactions allows reuse of the same register operation sequences, even if the specification changes to use a different bus. The bus interface is extended to support register sequence operations using the factory.

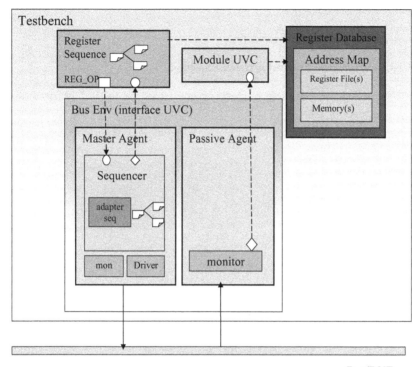

Bus/DUT

Figure 6-2: Testbench Instantiation and Connection

Testbench top file import the uvm package, uvm register package, register definition files of all IP's, sequence library file of all IP's, address map file, test file etc.

Testbench top file contains the instance of control and data bus UVC virtual interface, instance of RTL top and control and data bus assertion based VIP (ABVIP) module. Control and data bus protocol checker module connects to DUT interfaces using virtual interface.

Self-Assessment Questions:

6. Give the significance of address map.

7. Explain the reuse of register operation sequences.

8. Control and data bus protocol checker module connects to DUT interface using _____.

7. Reference Models

Structure

7.1 Introduction

Reference model in imaging group is Unified and Modular algorithms & ISP's modeling framework used for different applications such as Algorithms development, Reference for HW implementation, Reference for FW implementation, Bit-true certification, ISP modeling, IQ tools & metrics, Demo to customers, Versioning control, External deliveries etc.

In this unit you will study about the basic setup of UVM based verification environment using C/Python reference models for IP/Subsystem/SoC level verification. Next in this unit, benefits of Unified Modeling Framework are described. At the end, the usage of reference model for bit accurate verification is described.

Objectives

After studying this unit, you will be able to:

- assess the importance of reference model
- understand the use of python map file

- understand the concept of the Bit Accurate Verification using reference model

7.2 IP & ISP development flow

As described in Figure 7-1, Image signal processing algorithms are developed and evaluated using Python models before RTL/FW implementation. Once the algorithm is finalized, Python models are used as a golden reference model for the IP and ISP (Image Signal Processor) RTL and FW development.

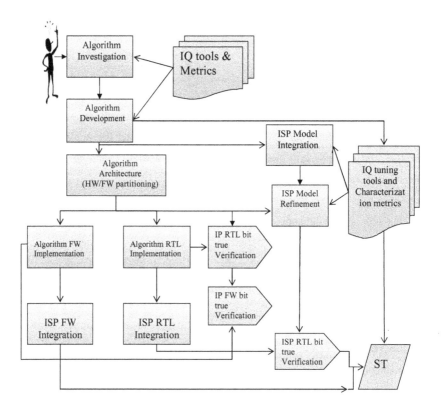

Figure 7-1: Algorithm development methodology from idea to product

Python reference models are used in System Verilog UVM based IP/Sub-system/SoC level Verification Environment for IP/ISP RTL bit true verification.

IP and ISP development flow is clearly understood from figure 7-2. At the start, the C/Python model is written for evaluation of the algorithms. At that stage, there is no hardware or firmware partitioning done in model. After evaluation, this model is used as a reference model for the algorithmic IP (by algorithmic we mean those IP's where image signal processing on the input image/data takes place). After evaluation stage, hardware and firmware portioning is done in reference model and an implementation model is developed where both HW and FW part of algorithm exists. Now FW part of this model is used by the firmware developer to verify the firmware drivers and HW part of python reference model is used at IP level for bit-true verification of the IP.

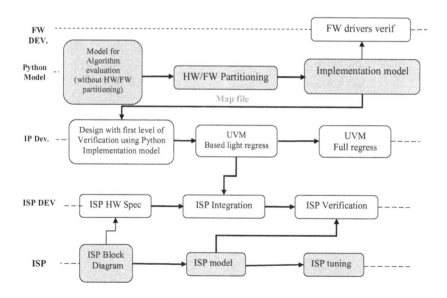

Figure 7-2: IP & ISP development flow

After initial verification of the IP by running few simulations, light regression is run using eManager (regression tool) so as to make sure 60-70 % of the IP has been verified and can be used for ISP RTL integration. Then full regression at IP level is run to complete Verification of the IP in parallel with initial verification of the ISP RTL at Subsystem/SoC level.

At ISP level, ISP block diagram represents ISP HW specifications. Verified IP's are integrated to make ISP system and ISP reference model is used for the verification. The ISP is then continued to be tuned for more improvements and better performance.

Mapping between RTL and reference model is provided through a Python map file with:

- A function which translates HW inputs (parameters, register values, memory contents and images) to model attributes,
- A function which translates model output attributes to HW outputs (register values, memory contents and images).
- Python mapping file describes how to transfer HW inputs to model inputs and model outputs to HW outputs, but neither describe how HW inputs have to be provided, nor how HW outputs have to be processed. Python script file provides those data and process the results.

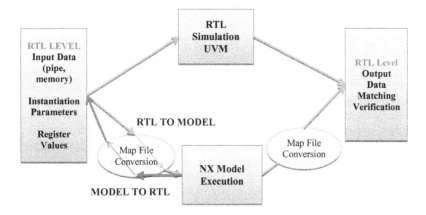

Figure 7-3: Bit-True Verification Overview

It is clear from the figure 7-3 that the map file contains both the RTL to model and model to RTL mapping. The most basic requirement to write a map file is to have the register description file and instantiation parameters description file. These files are in .xml format, so that they are easily converted to python map file via IPXACT flow.

7.2.1 Benefits of Unified Modeling Framework

Unified and Modular algorithms & ISP's modeling framework provides following benefits -

- Reduce development time
- Coherent modeling approach making development and support not reserved to algorithms experts
- Maximum IP re-use
- Traceability from product cut number to algorithm release number
- Bit-true certification between models and products
- Algorithms/ISP developers, HW designers, FW engineers, application and marketing guys are all speaking the same language!

Self-Assessment Questions:

1. Explain how reference model is used in UVM based verification environment?

2. What are benefits of Unified Modeling Framework?

3. Mapping between RTL and reference model is provided through _____ file.

4. What information does python map file provide?

7.3 Bit Accurate Verification using reference model

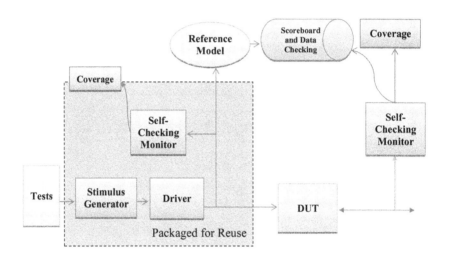

Figure 7-4: Bit Accurate Verification

Figure 7-4 shows the UVM based Verification Environment, where Python models are used as reference models for RTL Verification. Both Python reference model and RTL are configured with the same configuration values and output of reference model and RTL is compared for checking bit-trueness between RTL and reference model.

For the purpose of data checking, the UVM based verification environment integrates the python reference model. For control IP's, System Verilog scoreboard is written. Output of python model is compared with the output of the RTL in data checkers which are part of System Verilog UVM based verification environment. The three main functions carried out in the scoreboard are transfer function (reference model), expected data storage mechanism and checking logic.

Self-Assessment Questions:

5. Explain how data checking is done?

---

8. Assertion Based Verification

Structure

8.1 Introduction

Assertion based verification (ABV) is a methodology in which designers use assertions to capture specific design intent and verify them. It can be done either through formal verification, simulation, or emulation, thereby verifying that the design correctly implements that intent.

In this unit you will study about the basic assertion based verification flow. Next in this unit you will be acquainted with the major application of Assertion Based VIP. The significance of usage of assertion based verification early in the design to catch bugs before start of simulation is described.

Objectives

After studying this unit, you will be able to:

- assess the importance of assertion
- understand the verification flow using assertion
- understand the basics of formal verification
- understand the major application of the assertion based VIP

8.2 Assertion Based Verification Flow

Assertions are active comments embedded with in the design code and Assertion can be written within or outside of the design code, seamlessly. For same reason, both designers and verifiers can use it, independently, if needed. The typical verification that includes the usage of assertion is shown in the figure 8.1.

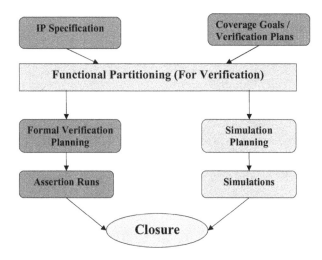

Figure 8-1: Typical Verification Flow including usage of assertions.

Assertion can be used to –

- Monitor signals on interface that connects different blocks. Improvement upon $display, $monitor and assert statements.
- Track expected behaviour of a logic gate, flip-flop or module.
- Watch for forbidden behaviour within a design block.

8.3 Static or Formal verification

Static or Formal verification means this analysis is static, hence no test bench or simulation are needed. This analysis starts from a single unique viz. after reset. Formal verification analyses the assertions in a design as true, false or indeterminate. In case the assertion is proven true, it guarantees 100% verification. It is effective for corner cases.

Static formal verification is usually performed at the block level.

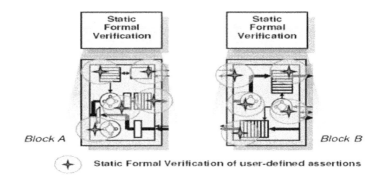

Figure 8-2: Static formal verification

Self-Assessment Questions:

1. What is Assertion Based Verification (ABV)? Give advantages of using ABV.

2. Explain static verification.

Formal analysis (FA) is a process that uses sophisticated algorithms to conclusively prove or disprove that a design behaves as desired for all possible operating states. Desired behavior is expressed as a set of assertions and not as a traditional testbench. Formal analysis does not need traditional user-developed test scenarios; instead it analyzes all legal input sequences concurrently and automatically.

UVM based Verification Environment – Theory and Practice

Formal analysis improves productivity and reduces time-to-market due to this automation feature. With formal analysis, many bugs can be found very early and quickly in the design process without the need to develop large sets of test scenarios or random test generators. In addition, due to its thorough nature, formal analysis, improves quality of the designs by finding corner-case bugs/issues, which are difficult to find from traditional verification (based on testbenches) methods. The dual benefits of increased productivity and increased quality are driving the usage of formal analysis into the design flows of many companies.

In formal analysis, properties are the basic units of expression. Properties are formalized statements about the behaviour of signals over time. They are expressed either through a property language, such as PSL, or a library of properties, such as OVL. Properties may express desired behaviour of a design under test or they may express the behaviour of the environment in which such a design is embedded. Properties, which express desired behaviour of a design under test, are called assertions. Properties, which express the behaviour of the environment, are called constraints. They are called constraints, because the presence of these properties constrains Formal Verifier to generate input sequences that satisfy the properties of the environment. Formal verification is complimentary for Simulation. Verification planning can be done keeping both Formal and simulation in mind. Enterprise Manager Tool can help in merging coverage. It is used early in the design cycle to catch bugs before start of simulation.

Assertion should be used in Control logic area like writing assertion in place of RTL comments, Block interfaces assertions, Queue/FIFO assertions, State machine assertions, Arbiter assertions, Use Global enable or disable for assertions etc.
Assertion should not be used in pure datapath logic area as the states may explode due to heavy datapath pipes.

8.4 Assertion Based VIP Application Examples

We are using static formal verification to compliment the Dynamic Metric Driven Verification methodology in IP/SoC verification. Static formal verification provide a substitute for some of the verification tasks usually done under dynamic simulation thus, reducing the regression re-runs to achieve coverage goals and to reduce the effort to write additional test scenarios. Some of the examples of Assertion Based VIP application in imaging group are as follows -

a) Protocol Compliance Checking

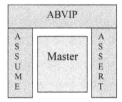

Figure 8-3: Protocol Compliance Checking

As described in figure 8.3, a top level module contains a Master IP and an assertion based VIP monitor. Master behavior of IP is checked with ABVIP master properties. Slave behavior is assumed with ABVIP slave properties.

b) As a driver (Constraints) to verify other functionality

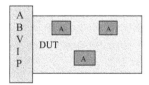

Figure 8-4: ABVIP as a driver (Constraints)

As described in figure 8.4, ABVIP drives defined, constrained random bus traffic to DUT following interface bus protocol to offload this time consuming task from dynamic simulation and to verify functionality of the RTL. Interface bus protocol behavior is assumed with ABVIP interface bus properties.

c) Protocol Conversion (bridge) Verification

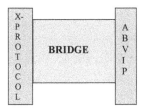

Figure 8-5: ABVIP for Protocol Conversion (bridge) Verification

As described in figure 8.5, ABVIP is used for verification of protocol conversion (bridge).Formal verification is very efficient way for verification of bridges. Using only dynamic simulations for verification of bridges cannot efficiently complete the full verification of Bridges as some test scenarios may miss in dynamic simulations.

d) As protocol Monitor in simulation provides also functional coverage

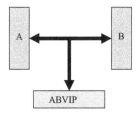

Figure 8-6: ABVIP as protocol Monitor

As described in figure 8.6, ABVIP is also used in dynamic simulations to monitor the bus protocol. ABVIP also provides functional coverage of the properties covered.

The verification environment uses following tools/VIPs:

- Incisive Formal Verifier (IFV) tool from Cadence
- PSL/SV based assertion libraries (VIP's) for standard protocols (AXI, AHB, APB etc.)
- PSL/SV based assertion libraries for imaging specific protocols

---

Self-Assessment Questions:

3. Assertion should be used in pure datapath logic. (True/False)

4. What are the advantages of using formal analysis?

5. Properties are expressed either through a property language or through a library of properties. Give an example of each.

6. Properties which express desired behaviour of a design under test are called _____.

7. Properties which express the behaviour of the environment are called _____.

---

9. Accelerated VIP

Structure

9.1 Introduction

    9.1.1 Objectives

9.2 Emulation and Co-emulation

9.3 Typical Verification VIP

9.4 TBX Technology with UVM Methodology

9.5 Simulation to Emulation Implementation

9.6 VRI Based Veloce Emulation Platform

9.1 Introduction

With increase of complexity at SoC level and Verification Environment, there is strong need to re-use as much possible from IP to SoC and also from Simulation to Emulation.

If we see what we used to do at SOC level verification, it was mainly Register map tests and simple IP data flow integration tests where one IP was active at a time, along with connectivity test.

Now in current complex and faster time frame, targeting Vanilla kind of testing is not sufficient as there is need to do multi-IP stress test where groups of IPs exchange data simultaneously, performance assessment with real application scenarios. Also, there is strong need to follow some metrics to conclude whether we have done or not even on Emulation because we cannot really run tests on Simulation. Hence support of Code Coverage, Functional Coverage, Assertions, and Low Power etc. is key.

In this unit you will study about the basics of accelerated VIP. The concept of emulation and co-emulation is described in detail. Next in this unit, you will be acquainted with the importance of emulation. Further in this unit, simulation to emulation implementation is described in detail with the help of sample example code. At the end, VRI based Veloce emulation platform is discussed.

Objectives

After studying this unit, you will be able to:

- assess the importance of accelerated VIP

- understand the emulation and co-emulation

- understand the Simulation to Emulation Implementation

- understand the basics of VRI Based Veloce Emulation Platform

9.2 Emulation and Co-emulation

Previously in chapter 4, typical SoC level Verification Environment has been covered, still I would like to mention again to refresh. Recall the part where we studied SoC level Functional Verification Environment using UVM. This is shown in figure 9.1.

So looking into this above mentioned verification setup, verifying this kind of complex design is not feasible on software Simulator so we have to use HW solution e.g. Emulator or FPGA prototype.

Since Emulation is very user friendly and easy to deploy so we in ST focusing on Emulation platform. Currently for most of projects, we are targeting Veloce Emulation machine which is capable to handle many complex and heterogeneous platform on HW Machine; thanks to TestBench XPress (TBX) methodology e.g.

SystemC, System Verilog UVM, Verilog/VHDL, external HW board along-with various solutions.

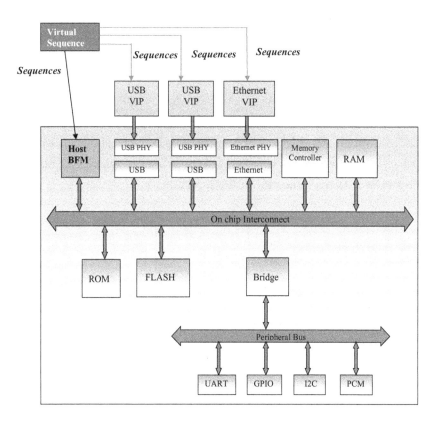

Figure 9-1: SoC level Functional Verification Env using UVM

As mentioned above Emulation is either FPGA or custom ASIC based HW platform which is target for faster verification. Since this kind of HW Emulator is supported by highly customized and efficient Software that make user's life very easy to run/debug any extremely complex Platforms.

In-Circuit-Emulation mode is a traditional way where testbench and DUT both are synthesizable and mapped on Hardware Emulator box to have faster performance. The same platform can be used by Software engineers for pre-silicon validation. Software debug connections to emulation have traditionally been handled using hardware-based, JTAG probe connections. Because JTAG uses a serial data connection, performance is limited on the emulator.

The term Co-emulation refers to platform where Testbench (which is Non-Synthesizable part) in HVL language mapped on Linux Host station while RTL Design (Synthesizable Part) in HDL Language mapped on Emulation machine and these two are communicated through Co-emulation channel which can be Standard Co-Emulation Modeling Interface (SCE-MI)/ SV DPI.

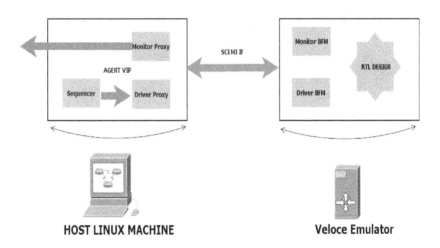

Figure 9-2: Co-emulation

In Cycle Accurate Co-emulation, the testbench is written and executed in HVL for greater testbench performance. Signals are synchronized at clock boundaries. Clocks advance under control of the HVL testbench. This approach makes complete system slower as there will always be interaction with Hardware and Software at each clock.

In Transaction-Level Co-Emulation, the testbench is written in SystemC, C++ or SystemVerilog. Packets of data (transactions) are exchanged between the testbench and the DUT. This reduces the communication time between the host machine and emulator as data transfers are performed in transaction level instead of signal level first approach. To do this, transactor should be described in a synthesizable way to mapped on hardware emulator with DUT. Moreover, the transactor design depends on both emulator system protocol and DUT protocol. Therefore, transactor description would not only be time-consuming but also error-prone task.

The Standard Co-Emulation Modeling Interface (SCE-MI) was first introduced at that time as a way to standardize the communication between the hardware portion running in the emulator and the software portion running on the Host Machine.

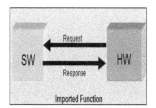 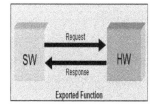

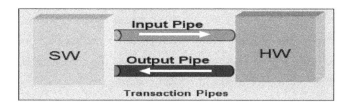

Figure 9-3: SCEMI-2 Infrastructure

Following are few important points to highlight Co-Emulation:

- Easiness of design mapping: No need of a user intervention to partition the design compare to traditional FPGA prototyping.
- Complete visibility of all the internal signals of the design: Emulators have equivalent debug capability provided by the RTL simulator. There are more debugging features enabled in Emulators like trigger based faster debugging, netlist debugging, save-restore, profile...
- Unique verification environment: Smooth path from simulation to emulation. Importantly it's also assured that the entire environment including the untimed UVM components and the timed transactors is a single source for both conventional simulation and for the co-emulation flow. Thus, any model functional on emulator can also be run in simulation alone using a SystemVerilog compliant simulator which eliminates the need to maintain separate models and environments.
- Efficient usage of an emulator: Regressions instead of just interactive usage mode.
- Enable simulation of modern complex SoCs Performance analysis on modern interconnect is currently challenging and test intensive so Emulation is key for this.
- Easiness to Debug: To monitor system bus activity and inter-block communication for improved debug visibility, there are SystemVerilog assertions inside the DUT and these are supported by Veloce/TBX for synthesis into the emulator. The real benefits of assertion-based verification with the high-performance of emulation significantly reduce the time to detect and resolve bugs.

Self-Assessment Questions:

1. What are Accelerated VIPs and how it's different from Simulation-based VIPs?

2. What are Emulation and Co-emulation and their importance in product life-cycle?

9.3 Typical Verification VIP

A traditional verification environment has both synthesizable and non-synthesizable components instantiated in a single testbench top, as shown in below Figure-9.4.

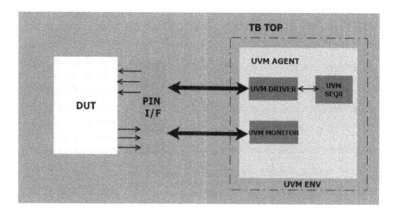

Figure 9-4: Traditional Verification Environment

This limits running the testbench in a co-emulation mode, where two different physical devices are involved: a Hardware Emulator and a Work Station.

A recommended guideline is to create an Acceleratable testbench that is partitioned into two tops:
TESTBENCH_HDL_TOP and TESTBENCH_HVL_TOP

TESTBENCH_HDL_TOP has all the synthesizable timed components instantiated in it. TESTBENCH_HVL_TOP contains all untimed behavioral components as shown in Figure-9.5.

Synthesized TESTBENCH_HDL_TOP runs on the hardware accelerator and TESTBENCH_HVL_TOP runs on the Host Linux machine. The HDL and HVL partitions of the setup communicate at the transaction level. This communication is enabled by virtual interface based tasks/functions.

TBX establishes a SCE-MI compliant, transaction-level communications link between testbenches running on a host system and SoC mapped on Veloce hardware emulation box.

Transaction-level verification is a verification methodology both in simulation and emulation. In emulation it is further leveraged due to the superior performance that it yields. Transactors are an important component in transaction-level verification, and serve as the bridge between a test environment written in a Hardware Verification Language (HVL) and the DesignUnderTest (DUT) inside the Veloce emulator. The Transactor is responsible for converting the high-level HVL commands into low-level DUT pin wiggles (HDL), and handling the communication between the two domains (HVL and HDL) (Figure 9-5).

A protocol transactor implements a protocol (AMBA, USB, ST Internal Protocol and so on) which drives the DUT interface in a protocol-compliant way, and captures DUT responses into high level protocol transactions.

Due to the high-level interface at the HVL side, the verification environment is free from modeling low-level protocol details, thus ensuring easy and more comprehensive test development. This transaction-level verification environment can now run at full emulation performance using Testbench-Xpress (TBX) and Veloce, without sacrificing much of the functional coverage of the protocol.

A virtual interface is a SystemVerilog variable that holds a reference to a concrete SystemVerilog interface instance. A variable of a virtual interface type can be assigned the hierarchical path name of the given interface instance in HDL_TOP. Currently veloce emulation platform supports a synthesizable transaction interface that provides communication between emulator and testbench. Transaction interfaces encapsulate synthesizable SystemVerilog tasks and functions. A driver calls a function or task using a reference to a synthesized SystemVerilog interface to access DUT pins and signals. Similarly, a monitor waits on a function call from a transaction interface. All accesses to DUT pins and signals are thus strictly confined to the HDL partition. All such functions and tasks are restricted to synthesizable data types.

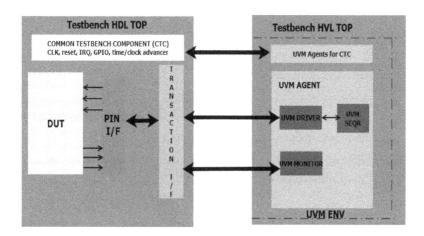

Figure 9-5: Transactor Bridging from HVL to HDL

Self-Assessment Questions:

3. In _____ mode, _____ testbench is recommended from EDA because two different physical devices are involved to run the environment compare to single testbench in _____.

9.4. TBX Technology with UVM Methodology

A transaction can be defined as a transfer of data from one component to another that may or may not consume time. In any procedural language like C, SystemC or SystemVerilog, a transaction is equivalent to a function call. TBX facilitates this through its support of remote procedure invocation, whereby, tasks or function calls defined on one domain could be called from the other.

For running on TBX, the environment must be partitioned into synthesizable XRTL compliant HDL files and the HVL files containing the high-level test bench components and compiled separately. So it will not be always needed to synthesize the HDL side which is time consuming.

Any transaction passed from HVL and HDL layers, via an xtf, must be packed into an equivalent static packed data structure that could be synthesized by TBX. Similarly, the XRTL will send a packed data structure that can be unpacked by the HVL to create transaction objects.

For such a scenario, it is best to divide the actual HVL transactor into a synthesizable XRTL transactor interface (tif) and a non-synthesizable proxy class. The tif can have a handle to the proxy class. The proxy class can contain a handle to the actual tif. The tif can call functions defined in the proxy, and the proxy can call functions or tasks defined in the tif.

9.5 Simulation to Emulation Implementation

A Simulation based VIP is a SystemVerilog interface driving a DUT interface (pin connections or SystemVerilog interface) on one side and connected to a test bench environment on the other side (like SV, OVM, or UVM), through a transaction-based set of APIs.

Figure 9.6 shows a typical Verification IP environment.

- Constrained random generation of protocol stimulus and driven through the API layer into the model. The model converts this high-level transaction into pin wiggles on the DUT interface.

- The model also captures responses from the interface (bus) and creates a high-level transaction the monitor recognizes on the test bench side. The monitor sends it to the various analysis ports where coverage and scoreboard modules are connected.

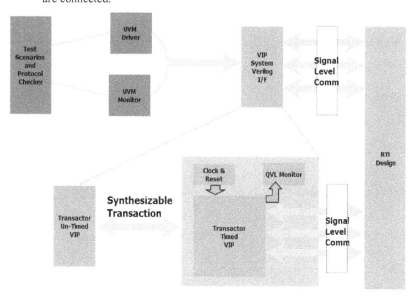

Figure 9-6: Comparison of Veloce Transactor to the Simulation Based VIP

Figure -9.6 gives a look for the Veloce Transactor comparison to the Simulation Based VIP. The verification environment in Veloce is in two domains: the XRTL (timed) portion of the transactor in Veloce, and the HVL (untimed) portion in the workstation (software). Models described using high-level language (HVL) constructs are executed by the simulator and the models described using hardware description language (HDL) constructs are executed by the hardware accelerator. Clocks and Reset are part of timed component and can be generated using TBX clkgen pragma which allow tool to synthesize this behavioral code and make it reside on Emulators.

A UVM agent generally contains sequencer, driver, and monitor.

A sequence item is a transaction object from the sequencer that stimulates the driver. In order to transfer a data item from the proxy in the HVL portion to the BFM in the HDL portion, the data members need to map into a packed struct Packet_t. Figure-9.7 shows the modeling of a sequence item Packet and a corresponding SystemVerilog packed struct Packet_t which represents synthesizable transaction of Packet.

```
`include "uvm_macros.svh"
class Packet extends uvm_sequence_item;
...
...
// Fields
  rand bit unsigned req;
  rand bit unsigned eop;
  rand bit [31:0] addr;
  rand bit [31:0] data;
  rand bit [3:0] be;
  bit unsigned r_req;
  bit [31:0] r_data;
  bit unsigned r_opc;
...
...
`uvm_object_utils_begin (Packet)

  `uvm_field_int (req, UVM_ALL_ON);
  `uvm_field_int (eop, UVM_ALL_ON);
  `uvm_field_int (addr, UVM_ALL_ON);
  `uvm_field_int (data, UVM_ALL_ON);
  `uvm_field_int (be, UVM_ALL_ON);
  `uvm_field_int (r_req, UVM_ALL_ON);
  `uvm_field_int (r_data, UVM_ALL_ON);
  `uvm_field_int (r_opc, UVM_ALL_ON);

`uvm_object_utils_end

function new (string name = "Packet");
super.new(name);
endfunction
endclass
```

```
Package Packet_t_pkg;
typedef struct packed {
  ...
  ...
  bit unsigned req;
  bit unsigned eop;
  bit [31:0] addr;
  bit [31:0] data;
  bit [3:0] be;
  bit unsigned r_req;
  bit [31:0] r_data;
  bit unsigned r_opc;
  ...
  ...
} Packet_t;
endpackage
```

Figure 9-7: Two Representations of Transaction

The class-based driver receives a sequence item, converts it to a SystemVerilog struct, and passes the transaction referred by a virtual interface. For conversion between the two representations (mentioned above), we need to declare function "from_class_to_struct" in driver class. In this model, the bus functional models (BFM) which are tasks/functions to drive DUT pins are implemented in a synthesizable SV Transactor interface. During the connect phase, the virtual interface of the UVM driver connects to a virtual interface BFM (in Figure-9.8) which, at the end of the elaboration step, connects to the actual transaction interface instance (driver_bfm_if).

```
import Packet_t_pkg::*;
class driver_proxy extends uvm_driver # (Packet);
Packet_t req_s;
//virtual driver_interface
virtual driver_bfm_if BFM;
......................

//build phase to get virtual interface
virtual function void build_phase (uvm_phase phase);
super.build_phase(phase);
uvm_config_db #(virtual driver_bfm_if)::get(this,"","driver_bfm_if",BFM);
if(BFM == null)
begin
`uvm_fatal("DRIVER_INTERFACE CONFIG ERROR", "driver_bfm_inf is
not set in driver proxy class");
end
endfunction

function Packet_t from_class_to_struct(Packet Packet_c);
  Packet_t Packet_t_s;
  Packet_t_s.req      =      Packet_c.req;
  Packet_t_s.eop      =      Packet_c.eop;
  Packet_t_s.addr     =      Packet_c.addr;
  Packet_t_s.data     =      Packet_c.data;
  Packet_t_s.be       =      Packet_c.be;
```

```
Packet_t_s.r_req       =      Packet_c.r_req;
Packet_t_s.r_data      =      Packet_c.r_data;
Packet_t_s.r_opc       =      Packet_c.r_opc;
return Packet_t_s;
endfunction

//execute the run phase
virtual task run_phase(uvm_phase pha    Interface driver_bfm_if ();
//BFM.wait_for_reset();                 //pragma attribute driver_bfm_if
forever                                 partition_interface_xif
begin                                   import Packet_t_pkg::*;
  seq_item_port.get_next_item(req);
  req_s = from_class_to_struct (req);   task drive (input stimulus_s my_packet
  BFM.drive(req_s);                     );//pragma tbx xtf
  seq_item_port.item_done();            @ (posedge clk);
...........................              begin
                                          req    = my_packet.req;
endclass                                  .................
                                        end
                                        endtask
                                        endinterface
```

Figure 9-8: Driver Proxy and Driver Interface

The synthesizable transaction interface (driver_bfm_if) contains functions and tasks to apply transaction packets to DUT pins. It contains tasks that a UVM driver uses to write the transaction item. Figure-9.8 shows the connection of an actual interface to a virtual interface and its connection to the driver.

Below is Monitor implementation (Figure 9-9) of a Control Bus UVC, where transaction interface (monitor_bfm_if) contains task to apply DUT pins into transaction item. Interface task have a proxy function call to transfer synthesizable transaction to proxy side monitor where proxy side uses conversion from System

Verilog struct to class sequence item type that can be further used for scoreboarding and other purposes.

```
import Packet_t_pkg::*;
class monitor_proxy extends uvm_monitor;
 Packet_t Packet_coll_s;
 Packet Packet_coll;
 //virtual monitor_interface
 virtual monitor_bfm_if BFM;
 uvm_analysis_port #(Packet) item_collected_port;
 ......................

 //build phase to get virtual interface
 virtual function void build_phase (uvm_
  super.build_phase(phase);
  uvm_config_db #(virtual
  monitor_bfm_if)::get(this,"","monitor_bf
  if(BFM == null)
  begin
   `uvm_fatal("MONITOR_INTERFACE
 is not set in driver proxy class");
  end
 endfunction

 virtual task run_phase(uvm_phase phase
  fork
  vif.collect_packet();
  join

 endtask : run_phase

 function void monitor_transaction (Pack
 Packet_coll = Packet::type_id::create("P
 Packet_coll.req    = Packet_coll_s.req;
 Packet_coll.eop    = Packet_coll_s.eop
 Packet_coll.addr   = Packet_coll_s.add
 Packet_coll.data   = Packet_coll_s.data
 Packet_coll.be     = Packet_coll_s.be;
 Packet_coll.r_req  = Packet_coll_s.r_re
 Packet_coll.r_data = Packet_coll_s.r_da
 Packet_coll.r_opc  = Packet_coll_s.r_o
 item_collected_port.write(Packet_coll);
 endfunction : monitor_transaction
```

```
Interface monitor_bfm_if ();
//pragma attribute monitor_bfm_if
partition_interface_xif
import Packet_t_pkg::*;
monitor_proxy proxy ; //HVL Monitor Class
definition
......................

task collect_packet(); //pragma tbx xtf
  Packet_t Packet_collected;
 @(posedge clk);

  forever begin
   wait(r_req == 1 );
   @(posedge clock);

   if(opc[0:0] == 0) begin
    packet_collected.addr = addr;
    packet_collected.be = be;
    packet_collected.eop = eop;
    packet_collected.req = req;
    packet_collected.data = data;
    ....................
   end
   ................

  proxy.monitor_transaction(packet_collected);
   end
  end
 endtask
 ......................
```

Figure 9-9: Monitor Proxy and Monitor Interface

The Virtual Interface Binding can be done easily at HVL top for concrete interface instances. This complete model is native SystemVerilog and hence works in any SystemVerilog compliant simulator.

```
module test;
import uvm_pkg::*;
`include "uvm_macros.svh"
`include "register_test.sv"

initial begin
 uvm_config_db#(virtual driver_bfm_if )::set(null, uvm_test_top.env.i_agent.drv",
"driver_bfm_if", testbench_hdl_top.DRIVER_BFM);
uvm_config_db#(virtual monitor_bfm_if )::set(null, "uvm_test_top.env.i_agent.mon",
"monitor_bfm_if", testbench_hdl_top.MONITOR_BFM);
run_test("register_test");
end
endmodule
```

Figure 9-10: Virtual Interface Binding

UVM_REG register and memory model is used to write register/memory sequences that access hardware registers and memory areas and thus, it is used as generator in verification environment and is independent of the DUT interface. UVM_REG Register and memory model is described using high-level language (HVL) constructs and is executed by the simulator.

To implement the unified testbench for simulation and acceleration, following coding guidelines are followed:

1- # Delays are not allowed in the testbench code.

2- To achieve best performance, all code on the HVL testbench side must be untimed, and all timed code should be synthesized.

3- There should not be any direct signal access from the HVL side. All communication must be transaction based.

Self-Assessment Questions:

4. What benefits Emulators have in compare to Simulators and traditional FPGA prototyping solutions?

5. Any model functional on Emulation will be functional on Simulation. TRUE/FALSE

6. Delays can be kept in HVL side in Co-Emulation. TRUE/FALSE

7. In Co-emulation, HVL side can access any signal directly from HDL. TRUE/FALSE

9.6 VRI Based Veloce Emulation Platform

As mentioned in Chapter 4, we can see from below picture how we mapped VRI based SV-UVM platform in Veloce Emulator .Here we use Mentor SV-PDI to have back-door access to Memory inside HW Emulator. While other Acceleratable VIP (AVIP) is communicating through Bus between HW and SW interfaces.

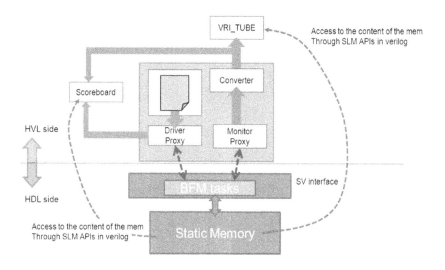

Figure 9-11: Example of the VRI-FE UVC in Co-Emulation

Self-Assessment Questions:

8. Explain Virtual Register Interface based SV-UVM platform in veloce emulator.

10. SystemC and Transaction Level Modeling

Structure

10.1 Introduction

    10.1.1 Objectives

10.2 SystemC

10.3 Transaction level Modeling

10.4 Image Signal Processor (ISP) designs and their Modeling

10.5 Flow used for design verification

10.1 Introduction

With semiconductor industry trend of "smaller the better", from an idea to a final product, more innovation on product portfolio and yet remaining competitive and profitable are few criteria which are culminating into pressure and need for more and more innovation for CAD flow, process management and project execution cycle. Project schedules are very tight and to achieve first silicon success is key, this necessitates quicker verification with better coverage matrix. Quicker Verification requires early development of the verification environment with wider test vectors without waiting for RTL to be available.

In this unit, you will study about the concept of SystemC language for system level modeling and transaction level modeling. Next in this unit, case study of ISP IP is discussed in detail. You will be able to understand the importance of the reuse of ISP TLM model in RTL verification environment. An improved multi-language verification flow is described, by addressing four major activities of verification –

1. Early creation of Executable specification

2. Early creation of Verification Environment

3. Early development of test vectors and

4. Better and increased Re-use of blocks

Objectives

After studying this unit, you will be able to:

- understand the basics of SystemC and TLM

- understand the modeling of Image Signal Processor IP

- assess the importance of reuse of ISP TLM model in RTL verification environment

- understand the basics of Virtual Processor Model with BFM

10.2 SystemC

SystemC is an open C++ class library for hardware modeling. SystemC provides a modeling framework for hardware systems in which high-level functional models can be refined down to the implementation in a single language, which given immense advantage in typical system design and development cycle. SystemC also enables modeling at high level of abstraction e.g. communication protocols, refinement to hardware, software modeling – interrupt, exception handling, hardware/software co-verification, system wide verification, IP exchange. SystemC provides almost all the advantages of Verilog and VHDL, concurrent processes e.g. methods, threads, concept of a clock, and wide variety of bit-true data types.

SystemC may be termed as a single, unified design and verification language that enables designers to express architectural and system-level attributes. One of the major advantages of SystemC is that it can be used to describe a system at several levels of abstraction, starting at a very high level of functional description and down to synthesizable Register Transfer Logic (RTL) style.

SystemC offers advantage of speed of faster model development (at any level of abstraction above RTL level), design and redesign cycle, faster and more productive architectural trade-off analysis, and ease of simulation as compared that of Verilog/VHDL.

10.2.1 Advantage of C++ Ecosystem

SystemC is not another C++ dialect, it is pure C++. Being C++, all tools and techniques, software engineering concept and methodologies can be applied for SystemC modeling as well, which are for C++. And the biggest advantage is speed of simulation.

SystemC comes with an inbuilt simulation kernel thus removing any dependency on any external tools requirement for simulation purpose. All tools – compiler, debugger, linting tools, profilers, IDE, SDK, etc. which can be used for C++ program development can be used for SystemC as well. Object oriented design flow, design patterns, UML (Unified Modeling Language) can be used for model development and refinement.

10.2.2 C++ Mechanism of SystemC

While C++ is certainly adequate for design of a huge or small software system, but it is not much sufficient for hardware modeling.

Some hardware-oriented features required in any language for representing real-world hardware scenarios were added in SystemC. SystemC evolved to give a meta-language like feel for hardware modeling. The major five hardware notions which are incorporated to achieve are:

1. Notion of time: modeling of time
2. HW data types: like fixed-point operation, 4-valued logic.
3. Concurrency: processes are defined and they execute in parallel in simulator
4. Module hierarchy to manage connectivity and structure

5. Management Communications between concurrent units of execution

Now these days, high level synthesis tools are maturing which are able to synthesis the SystemC model. Thus they are giving the advantage of using SystemC from Architecture exploration to synthesis phase of design evolution.

10.2.3 SystemC and Modeling

SystemC does not impose a bottom-up or top-down or even middle-out design flow. It is recognized fact that most design flows are iterative, and that it is rare that all components within a system are modelled at same level of abstraction.

SystemC is well capable of representing real-world implementation of hardware system. It supports structural accuracy – structure of the actual implementation, timing accuracy – timing of actual implementation which may arise because of constraints imposed by design specification and delays within the each processing elements of the system, functional accuracy – which is one of the corner stone for modeling, data organization accuracy and communication protocol accuracy – the correctness of agreement of communication between the initiator and target components reflecting the actual communication protocol used within the target implementation.

SystemC is well capable for developing executable specification – direct translation of design specification into SystemC completely independent of any proposed implementation, untimed functional model – similar to executable specification but no time delays, timed functional model – timing delays are added to processes within the design to reflect the timing constraints of the specification and processing delays of a particular target implementation.

Within a single language framework of SystemC, the major tasks which can be performed are:

- to develop and simulate complex system specification,
- to refine system specification to mix software and hardware implementations
- to accurately model hardware implementation all the way to the register transfer level.
- to easily represent complex data types using fixed-point numeric and integer types.
- to leverage extensive knowledge, infrastructure and code base build around C and C++.

Any model of computation can be broadly defined on following criteria:

- The model of time employed (untimed, integer-valued, real-valued) and the event ordering constraints within the system (unordered, partially ordered, globally ordered).
- The method(s) of connection between concurrent processes.
- The rules for process activation.

Notion of time in SystemC is represented in absolute and integer-values format. In SystemC we can model virtually any discrete time system. Some of these systems may be:

- Static Multi-rate Data-flow
- Dynamic Multi-rate Data-flow
- Kahn Process Networks
- Communicating Sequential Processes
- Discrete Event as used for
    a. RTL hardware modeling
    b. Network modeling (e.g. waiting-room models)
    c. Transaction level modeling of SoC platform

A typical flow of SystemC model development can be depicted in following diagram.

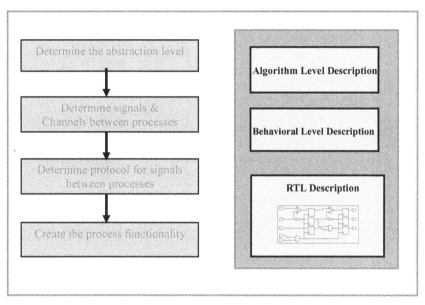

Figure 10-1: Typical System Development flow

10.2.4 SystemC Language Architecture

SystemC uses layered framework architecture approach which allows for the flexibility of introducing new, high-level constructs that share an efficient simulation engine. The base layer of SystemC provides an event-driven simulation kernel which works with events and processes in abstract manner. The kernel knows only how to operate on events and switch between processes, without knowing that the events actually represent or what the process do. In brief, few important concepts of SystemC Core Library can be summarized in figure 10-2 [11].

- Complete SystemC is built on C++

- SystemC core language provides only minimal set of modeling constructs for structural description, Concurrency, communication, and synchronization.
  - Works with events and process
  - Channels and Interfaces are used to describe communication.
  - Consists of an event-driven simulator as the base,
  - Consists of modules and ports for representing structure
- Data types are separate from the main core language and user-defined data types are fully supported.
- Commonly used communication mechanisms such as signals and fifos can be built on top of the core language. Commonly used models of computation (MOCs) can also be built on top of the core language.
- When desired, lower layers within the diagram can be used without needing the upper layers.

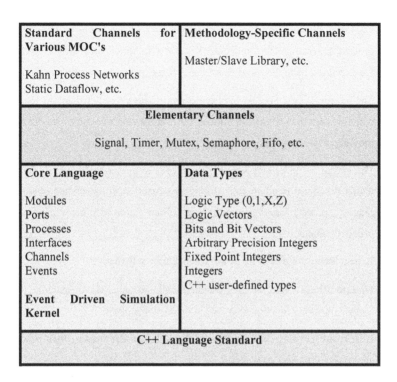

Standard Channels for Various MOC's	Methodology-Specific Channels
Kahn Process Networks Static Dataflow, etc.	Master/Slave Library, etc.

Elementary Channels
Signal, Timer, Mutex, Semaphore, Fifo, etc.

Core Language	Data Types
Modules Ports Processes Interfaces Channels Events	Logic Type (0,1,X,Z) Logic Vectors Bits and Bit Vectors Arbitrary Precision Integers Fixed Point Integers Integers C++ user-defined types
Event Driven Simulation Kernel	

C++ Language Standard

Figure 10-2: SystemC language architecture

10.2.5 SystemC Simulation Semantics

1. **Initialization Phase:** Each method process is executed once during initialization and each thread process is executed until a wait statement is encountered.

   The order of execution of processes is unspecified. The order of execution between processes is deterministic. Which shows that two simulation runs using the same version of the same simulator must yield identical results. However, different versions or a different simulator may yield a different result if care is not taken when writing models

2. Evaluate Phase. From the set of processes that are ready to run, select a process and resume its execution. The order in which processes are selected for execution from the set of processes that are ready to run is unspecified.

The execution of a process may cause immediate event notifications to occur, which in turn may trigger additional set of processes becoming ready to run in the same evaluate phase.

The execution of a process may include calls to the request_update() function which schedules pending calls to update() function in the update phase. The request_update() function may only be called inside member functions of a primitive channel.

3. Repeat Step 2 for any other processes that are ready to run.

4. Update Phase: Execute any pending calls to update() from calls to the request_update() function executed in the evaluate phase.

5. If there are pending delta-delay notifications, then determine which processes are ready to run and go to step 2.

6. If there are no more timed event notifications, then the simulation is finished.

7. Else, advance the current simulation time to the time of the earliest (next) pending timed event notification.

8. Determine which processes become ready to run due to the events that have pending notifications at the current time. After that, go to step 2.

Self-Assessment Questions:

1. What are benefits of using SystemC?

2. List some of the features of SystemC libraries which are not available in C++.

3. The order of execution of processes is _____. The order of execution between processes is _____.

4. Two simulations that run using the same version of the same simulator must yield identical results. (True/False)

5. Which simulation tool is used for SystemC model simulation?

10.3 Transaction Level Modeling

The future of system design, especially System-on-Chip (SoC), can be well characterized by the trend in semiconductor industry - "the smaller the better". Continuously more and more pressure to master the SoC design complexity within short project schedule limits the full exploitation of new silicone capabilities. This limiting factor is continuously pushing the need for altering the classic SoC design flow in prominence. Because of the complexity of managing an advanced SoC development process has evolved a novel SoC design flow starting from a higher abstraction level than RTL, i.e. System-to-RTL design flow. After a decade of attempts to define a useful intermediate abstraction between SoC paper specification and synthesizable RTL, the SystemC C++ open-source class library has finally emerged as the right vehicle to explore the adequate level of abstraction. A methodology - Transaction Level Modeling (TLM), , based on higher level of abstraction, has proven revolutionary values in bringing hardware and software teams together using the unique reference model; resulting in dramatic reduction of time-to-market and improvement of SoC design quality.

Transaction level modeling (TLM) is put forward as a promising solution above Register Transfer Level (RTL) in SoC design flow. TLM also eases task of SoC design activities ranging from architecture analysis and functional verification to early software development. The most rewarding benefit of TLM is the real hardware/software co-design founded on a unique reference, giving advantage of reduced time-to-market and comprehensive cross-team design methodology.

TLM would help to increase the productivity of architects, implementation, verification engineers and software engineers. In order to achieve the maximum benefit of improvement in productivity as promised by such a methodology, there is strong need to standardize the concept.

And the standard must address following issues. Some features which must have are:

- It should be easy, efficient and safe to use in a concurrent environment.
- It should enable reuse between projects and between abstraction levels within the same project.
- It should easily model hardware, software and designs which cross the hardware /software boundary.
- It should enable the design of generic components such as routers and arbiters.

Embedded Software: One of the most important targets of TLM platform methodology is of early embedded software development, testing, integration and validation. Early TLM gives great benefits to software designers and software designers gives early feedback to hardware designers from software point of view. So, in a way we may say that TLM platform can be considered as the meeting point between hardware and software development teams.

Functional Verification: Functional verification has traditionally focused on providing tools to generate tests and measuring their so-called coverage. However, there is lack of attention in providing correct reference data. TLM models can be considered as executable functional specifications to generate the compulsory reference data required by functional verification environments. Such models can easily be used in conjunction with other verification techniques such as hardware emulators, formal verification techniques.

Transaction-level modeling (TLM) is a technique for describing a system by using function calls that define a set of transactions over a set of channels.

TLM descriptions can be more abstract (as the use case is), and therefore it simulates more quickly than the register-transfer level (RTL) descriptions more traditionally used as a starting point for IC implementations. On other side, TLM can still be used to define designs in a less abstract, more detailed way. Now these days, industry is increasingly using it to encapsulate existing detailed functional block descriptions, creating consistent frameworks (a.k.a 'virtual platforms'), for integrating and simulating various components in system designs that are evolving at many levels of abstraction.

TLM gives designers a consistent way to model transactions in systems based on a memory-mapped bus architecture scheme. The resultant virtual platforms should be functionally complete and accurate at the register level, but yet lack the clocks, signal pins, and implementation details which lesser abstract modeling techniques use, and because of which it slow down simulation. The timing of the TLM model will be loose or approximate.

Layered Abstraction of TLM: TLM definition is based on three layers.

1. Layer-1 : the lowest layer involves 'mechanisms', which are C++ application programming interface (APIs) that define functions such as blocking and non-blocking interfaces, sockets, direct memory interfaces, generic payload, phases and more, and which ensures interoperability.
2. Layer-2: This layer offers two guidelines for coding styles that define how loosely timed and approximately timed TLM blocks are written.
3. Layer-3: The third and highest layer of TLM are four use-cases:
    a. software development,
    b. software performance estimation,
    c. architectural analysis and performance modeling,
    d. Hardware verification.

Although TLM seem like one level of abstraction (ESL), there are more abstractions within this one level. The table given below gives an idea of how different levels of coding styles are used for different abstraction levels of modeling to address uses cases. And following graphs also depicts the relation between accuracy and simulation performance.

1. **Untimed:** The untimed models do not have any notion of time and different Processes run at a pre-determined synchronization points.

2. **Loosely-timed models**: These kinds of models have two timing points - transaction start and end points. Models use blocking calls for communication between modules. This kind of coding style is mostly utilized for virtual platform development and software performance analysis. Models keep just enough information such that we are able to run operating systems and handle multicore systems. In order to accelerate simulation, models uses mechanism of bypassing the transaction-based block-to-block interface entirely and make direct access to areas of memory within a target function, and models are allowed to run ahead of the master simulation clock.

3. **Approximately timed models**: Such kinds of models have multiple timing points. Timed event notifications mechanisms are used to annotate delays. Non-blocking function calls are used which have multiple phases and explicit timing points for phase transition. Performance exploration is a typical use case for this style of coding. Such models add just enough timing information to make the model useful for architectural exploration and performance analysis and it run in lockstep with the master simulation clock.

4. **Cycle accurate:** Cycle accurate models can be implemented by extending the phases and timing points in the approximately timed models. This enables the model to be able to accurately model protocol mapping from RTL to TLM. Cycle accuracy can be achieved through ignorable extensions. Since there can be many implementations for modeling hardware, cycle accurate modeling cannot be standardized.

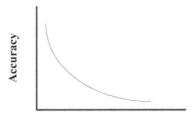

Simulation Performance

Figure 10-3: Accuracy and simulation Speed trade-off

Table 1: Use cases (coding style) in TLM modeling

Use Case	Coding Style
Software Application Development	Loosely-timed
Software Performance Analysis	Loosely-timed
Hardware Architectural Analysis	Loosely-timed or Approximately-timed
Hardware Performance Verification	Approximately-timed or Cycle Accurate
Hardware Functional Verification	Untimed, Loosely-timed or Approximately-timed

Self-Assessment Questions:

6. What are benefits of using TLM?

7. Explain the layered abstraction of TLM.

8. Use of loosely-timed models speeds up simulation. (True/False)

10.4 Image Signal Processor (ISP) designs and their Modeling

Image signal processors (ISP) address different markets, including high-end smartphones, security/surveillance, gaming, automotive and medical applications. The use of industry standard interfaces and rich set of APIs makes the integration of image processors a straightforward process and helps to reduce end-product time to market.

10.4.1 Modeling of ISP designs

A loosely timed high level model of the ISP block is generated at algorithmic functional level using C/C++/SystemC and with TLM-2 interface.

The SCML – SystemC Modeling Library, an open source SystemC library from Synopsys Inc. (www.synopsys.com) is being used here.

The purpose of this model generation is to use this model as a reference model. We may say it as a "Golden Reference Model" or "Executable Functional Specification" of the ISP designs. From functional and structural perspective this model can be divided in two major spaces.

First space - the algorithmic computational part, is mainly responsible for image processing using various algorithms involved for image manipulation from the incoming image stream data.

The second part – a TLM interface, is responsible for all kinds of communication to external IPs and other system blocks.

Register interface of this model is generated using IP-XACT tools. And algorithmic part is manually implemented.

10.4.2 Testing of Executable Spec only

To test the model, an environment is developed using Python (an open source scripting language) and Synopsys Pa-Virtualizer Tool Chain.

The test environment has following major components:

- Test bench in Python
- Configuration file reader in Python
- Raw Data Reader
- ISP model
- Input data injector in Python
- Output data receiver in Python
- Output data checker in Python
- Synopsys Pa-Virtualizer Tools Chain for GUI, debugging, and simulation

XML file format is used for test bench configuration and passing other parameter to testing environment.

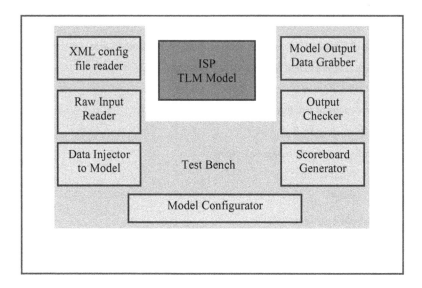

Figure 10-4: ISP model testing environment

10.4.3 Use of TLM model for early development of RTL verification environment

After the ISP model is proved to be functionally correct, the same model is used to early develop RTL functional verification environment.

A suitable TLM sub-system is designed. This TLM sub-system consists of ISP functional model, AXI BFM, configurable clock generators model, configurable reset generator model, memory model, configurable interconnect etc. All these are pure SystemC models. AXI BFM is provided to interact with other world.

ISP RTL block needs exhaustive verification. But, verification can only be possible when the RTL is ready. But, development of RTL design takes time, which means verification of RTL design can't be possible before it becomes available. To shorten this sequential activity, functional model of ISP is used to prepare the early verification environment.

A SystemVerilog test bench wrapper is created over SystemC/TLM ISP sub-system. This SystemVerilog test bench interface with the RTL verification environment.

10.4.4 Virtual Platform Sub-system

When all components of platform are in TLM/C, means C/C++ are used as modeling language; we call it a Pure Virtual platform. In typical verification environment, generally all verification components are not only TLM based but also of different verification languages thus making it a Multi-language heterogeneous simulation environment. For developing early verification environment, TLM based sub-system is developed which consists of every block in TLM/C. This TLM based Sub-system is model of RTL.

In the above mentioned RTL verification environment, a processor model is used which enables us to early develop 'C' test cases for programming of RTL registers/memories via CPU interface. The challenge is to keep the verification environment independent of "C" test cases. We don't wish to compile every time whenever there is change in application code.

To be able to achieve this, a sub-system is designed which consists of models of bus interfaces, like AXI/AHB BFM, a "generic" processor model, model of memory, etc. an independent "C" program/test case is written to do all the programming and configuration, which in turn runs on processor model of this sub-system. This sub-system is active element in programming phase, but becomes passive once the programming is complete.

Virtual platform sub-system can be represented in following block diagram.

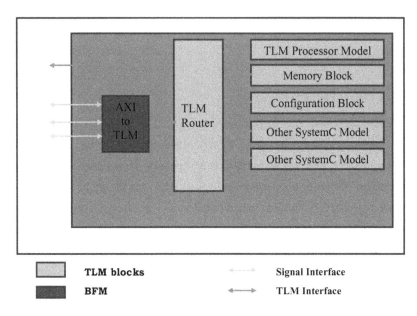

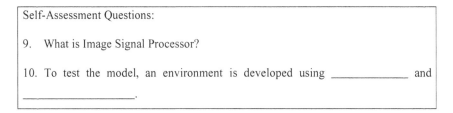

| TLM blocks | Signal Interface |
| BFM | TLM Interface |

Figure 10-5: Virtual Platform Sub-system

Self-Assessment Questions:

9. What is Image Signal Processor?

10. To test the model, an environment is developed using _____ and

_____.

10.5 Flow used for design verification

Much before arrival of RTL, C/Python model of image signal processor designs is developed for algorithm evaluation. Then, TLM/SystemC model of the design is created/generated from C/Python model. After proper exhaustive validation of the model with required test vectors, the model qualifies as an Executable Golden Model or Executable Specification means a 'living' benchmark for design specification. Enabling the use of TLM Model as DUT expedites development and better proofing of the verification environment with wider test vectors without waiting for RTL to be available.

Standard 'interfaces' are used to enable the reuse of verification components. In addition to standard method of bus-interface or signals level connectivity, UVM Multi-Language Open Architecture is used to connect System Verilog TLM port directly to SystemC TLM port which gives advantage of better simulation speed and better development/debug cycle in addition of clean, better and easy connectivity/integration of blocks. Presence of TLM components gives us flexibility to make backdoor direct access to the DUT registers and memories.

A processor model is used which enables us to early develop 'C' test cases for programming of RTL registers/memories via CPU interface. Same 'C' test cases are used for controlling the System Verilog UVC's using Virtual Register interface (VRI) layer. In our verification environment, we also have alternative Host interface path to do programming of configurable blocks using System Verilog UVM based test cases and in both cases control/data flows across TLM and bus interface boundaries. This method enhances the chances of re-using different already existing blocks in flow. IP-XACT based tools are also used for automatically configuring the environment for various IPs/SoCs.

By the time RTL arrives, complete verification environment and test-vectors are ready with sufficient sanctity, thus eliminating the number of verification environment issues which may arise when actual RTL verification is started. When RTL arrives, the TLM/SystemC model is simply replaced with RTL block with reuse of maximum of other verification components, which enhances the rapid/regress testing of design immediately. Also same C test cases have been run on actual core.

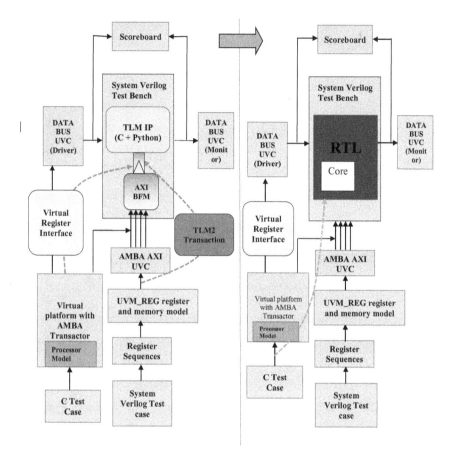

Figure 10-6: Reuse of early developed Verification environment

Self-Assessment Questions:

11. Explain the Flow used for design verification.

12. What is role of Virtual Register Interface (VRI) layer?

11. Regressions and Coverage Analysis

Structure

11.1 Introduction

Enterprise Manager is used for running regressions and coverage analysis. Enterprise Manager facilitates the basic, every-day tasks of verification process like Launching thousands of runs in a single session using a distributed resource manager, Facilitating failure analysis by automatically extracting, filtering, and grouping key information from all log files in one or more sessions. It can also launch the rerun of failed tests in debug mode and manage failure scenarios and it facilitates coverage and assertion analysis by presenting data gathered by multiple agents (Incisive Simulator, Incisive Formal Verifier, and Specman) in the same window, also creates HTML reports and creates progress chart and report, gives low power verification, Verification planning with Enterprise Planner, and also it gives advanced coverage analysis and vplan refinement tools.

In this unit you will study about the basics of Incisive Enterprise Manager. Next in this unit, internal verification flow for efficient setup of simulations and regressions is described in detail.

Objectives

After studying this unit, you will be able to:

- understand the use of Enterprise Manager

- understand the Verification Cockpit flow

11.2 Incisive Enterprise Manager

Incisive enterprise manager is a tool to manage the regression. Using this tool more than one test case with different attributes can be run in a single session. Tests are specified in verification session input format (.vsif) file. This tool helps in reducing the time for testing every single test case for different attribute or parameter. It can also provide results for both functional and code coverage.

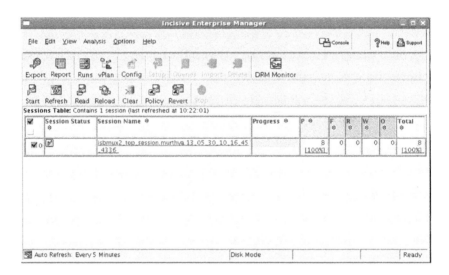

Figure 11-1: Enterprise Manager Window

Once all the tests have been passed then vPlan gives the coverage analysis. It is shown in figure 11-2.

UVM based Verification Environment – Theory and Practice

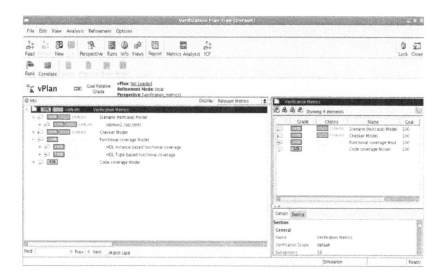

Figure 11-2: vPlan for Coverage

Self-Assessment Questions:

1. Why do we use Enterprise Manager?

2. In which file tests are specified?

3. When do we use vPlan?

11.3 Verification Cockpit

Verification cockpit is a ST internal framework which allows the user to concentrate more on debugging design issues rather than debugging tool integration and script maintenance issues. Main properties of Verification cockpit are -

- Verification Cockpit is a Linux compatible product which has been installed and used in ST.

- It is an infrastructure tool that bridges other tools such as NCsim, Enterprise Manager etc.

The main backbone of verification cockpit is 2 scripts –

- Testcase(s) description file (testcase.csv) which describes list of all test cases in the Environment with attributes like timeout etc.

- Setup script (vc_setup.csh) which sets the entire variable used in the environment.

```
TEST_NAME, TOPFILES, TIMEOUT, COUNT
streaming_generic_test,streaming_generic_test,1000000,1
uvm_reg_hw_reset_seq_test,uvm_reg_hw_reset_seq_test,1000000,1
uvm_reg_single_bit_bash_test,uvm_reg_single_bit_bash_test,1000000,1
uvm_reg_bit_bash_test,uvm_reg_bit_bash_test,1000000,1
uvm_reg_single_access_seq_test,uvm_reg_single_access_seq_test,1000000,1
uvm_reg_access_seq_test,uvm_reg_access_seq_test,1000000,1
uvm_reg_mem_access_seq_test,uvm_reg_mem_access_seq_test,1000000,1
uvm_reg_shared_access_seq_test,uvm_reg_shared_access_seq_test,1000000,1
uvm_mem_shared_access_seq_test,uvm_mem_shared_access_seq_test,1000000,1
```

Figure 11-3: Testcases description file

The steps for setup of these files are as follow:

1. The user need to create the Verification Environment setup script file in which all the variables are listed which points to the certain directories and scripts used in the Environment.

2. The Verification Cockpit setup file should also be pointed in the Verification Environment setup script file so that it will be invoked.

3. User need to create the testcases description file using the generic command with all the testcases names and their attributes in it.

11.4 Verification Cockpit Flow

The verification cockpit flow is described below:

11.4.1. Build and Compile:

Once the IP environment is set, first thing to do is to build the design. In order to build the design, build command is used. This command is invoked in the directory pointed by variable $VE_BUILD_DIR and will execute a script pointed by variable $VE_BUILD_SCRIPT. This variables are already been set in the verification cockpit setup file.

After the successful build, next step is to compile the design. To compile the IP environment compilation command are used. Compilation script is generally list of steps that the verification engineer uses for compilation. During compilation, if any error occurs, it can be viewed in the log file which will be generated in directory pointed by variable $VE_BUILD_DIR.

11.4.2. Running Standalone Test case:

After compiling the RTL and Verification Environment, simulation is carried out with any available simulator. Verification Cockpit have the setup available to use any simulator like ncsim, questasim, vcs etc. for running simulations.

Verification Cockpit Test runners can be customized for almost all kinds of Verification environment. Now at this stage, test cases as described in verification plan are run. Initially, built-in register test-cases as described in section-6.3 are run to verify the RTL register/memory configuration and then the streaming tests are run. The command to run the test-cases are launched in the directory pointed by variable $VE_RUN_DIR and executes a script pointed by variable $VE_TEST_RUNNER. These variables are already been set in the verification cockpit setup file. A tcl script is used for probing the DUT signals. The script has various options available for running the test. The results of simulation can be observed and the waveforms can be checked for verifying the functionality of the IP.

11.4.3. Running Regression

The Enterprise Manager Tool is used for running regressions.
For running regressions, Verification Cockpit generates .vsif file from the test-case description file and this generated .vsif file is input for the Enterprise Manager tool. The main aim over running regression is to have the coverage information such as function coverage, code coverage etc. of the IP/SoC been verified.

Verification Cockpit built-in scripts converts Test case description file into .vsif file.

Figure 11-4: Regression

11.4.4. Customize Regression

To run customized regression, vc_server command of Verification Cockpit is used –

1. This command invokes a terminal and provides a link to open in favourite web browser (Internet Explorer or Google Chrome etc...).
2. This opens a GUI based interface of the test-case description file where selection of the number of testcase(s) to be run is done. Also dumping of a VSIF file for running later or checking of status of runs on GUI window can be done.
3. Standalone test-case can be run from the GUI either in the same run directory or in new directory.
4. Probes can be enabled to run standalone test-case.
5. Filtering can be applied in case we have huge number of testcase and can save the filter to apply it whenever needed.
6. Regression can be run on a SQL server for which server setting has to be done on the verification cockpit setup.csh script and then the results can be extracted by pinging the SQL server and have a report as required.

Self-Assessment Questions:

4. Name two main backbone scripts for Verification Cockpit.

5. Explain the Verification Cockpit flow in detail.

6. For running regression, which is the input file to Enterprise Manager and how is this file generated?

---

12. Summary

The electronic industry grows by satiating a thirst for innovative features, performance and connectivity with new and unique products. Ever increasing silicon design complexity and transistor density, product differentiation and time to market are major factors creating huge pressure on complete design flow. The Accellera Universal Verification Methodology (UVM) arose in this environment as a means for large, distributed project teams to co-ordinate projects that spill across multiple companies and across geographies in an awesome display of engineering process and rapid standardization.

The chapters of this book provide our (imaging group) experiences that do just that - leverage the UVM to offer answers to the advanced topics facing verification teams.

The chapters of this book covered Generic and Reusable Universal Verification Methodology (UVM) based verification environment for efficient verification of imaging Sensor/Co-processor designs both with Host BFM and actual Core using Incisive Software Extension (ISX) and Virtual Register Interface (VRI) approaches. IP-XACT based tools are described for the automatic generation of IP/SoC dependent verification environment files. Usage of the UVM_REG register model to ease efficient verification of registers and memories is described. Significance of usage of assertion based verification early in the design to catch bugs before start of simulation is described. Usage of TLM/SystemC reference model of the design to enable the early development of Verification Environment without waiting for RTL to be available is described. Also extension of the standard simulation-only UVM to include hardware acceleration to make verification of chips more productive is described. This verification environment has been used for the verification of imaging IPs/SoCs.

Although this book covers verification environment which is developed for imaging Sensor/Co-processor designs. Same concept can be extended for verification of non-imaging designs. This book provides complete description of advanced verification environment for better verification of larger complex designs.

- Abhishek Jain

References

[1] Abhishek Jain, Giuseppe Bonanno, Dr. Hima Gupta and Ajay Goyal, (2012) "Generic System Verilog Universal Verification Methodology Based Reusable Verification Environment for Efficient Verification of Image Signal Processing IPs/SOCs", International Journal of VLSI Design & Communication Systems 2012.

[2] Abhishek Jain, Piyush Kumar Gupta, Dr. Hima Gupta and Sachish Dhar, (2013) "Accelerating System Verilog UVM Based VIP to Improve Methodology for Verification of Image Signal Processing Designs Using HW Emulator", International Journal of VLSI Design & Communication Systems 2013.

[3] Abhishek Jain, Mahesh Chandra, Arnaud Deleule and Saurin Patel, (2009) "Generic and Automatic Specman-based Verification Environment for Image Signal Processing IPs", Design & Reuse 2009.

[4] Rich Edelman et al., (2010) "You Are in a Maze of Twisty Little Sequences, All Alike – or Layering Sequences for Stimulus Abstraction", DVCON 2010.

[5] Jason Andrews, (2007) "Unified Verification of SoC Hardware and Embedded Software", Chip Design Magazine 2007.

[6] Mark Glasser, (2009) Open Verification Methodology Cookbook, Springer 2009.

[7] Iman, S., (2008) "Step-by-Step Functional Verification with SystemVerilog and OVM", Hansen Brown Publishing, ISBN: 978-0-9816562-1-2.

[8] Rosenberg, S. and Meade, K., (2010) "A Practical Guide to Adopting the Universal Verification Methodology (UVM)", Cadence Design Systems, ISBN 978-0-578-05995-6.

[9] J. Bergeron, (2003), "Writing Testbenches: Functional Verification of HDL models", Kluwer Academic Publishers, 2003.

[10] N. Kitchen and A. Kuehlmann, (2007) "Stimulus generation for constrainted random simulation", In International Conference on Computer-Aided Design, pages 258–265, 2007.

[11] Stuart Swan, (2001) "An Introduction to System Level Modeling in SystemC 2.0", Cadence Design Systems, Inc. May 2001

[12] Adam Rose, Stuart Swan, John Pierce, Jean-Michel Fernandez, (2005) "Transaction Level Modeling in SystemC", Cadence Design Systems, Inc.

[13] Frank Ghenassia, (2010) "Transaction Level Modeling with SystemC - TLM Concepts and Applications for Embedded Systems", ISBN: 978-0-387-26232-1.

[14] Daniel D. Gajski, (2003) "System-Level Design Methodology", www.cecs.uci.edu/~gajski.

[15] Lukai Cai and Daniel Gajski, (2003) "Transaction Level Modeling: An Overview", {lcai, gajski}@cecs.uci.edu

[16] Farooq Khalid Chughtai, (2012) "Accurate Performance Exploration of System- on-Chip using TLM".

[17] Thorsten, (2002) "System Design with SystemC", Kulwar Academic Publishers Group, 2002.

[18] Accellera Organization, Inc. Universal Verification Methodology (UVM) May 2012.

[19] Cadence Design Systems, Inc. Universal Reuse Methodology (URM).

[20] Cadence Design Systems, Inc. Open Verification Methodology Multi-Language (OVM-ML).

[21] IEEE Computer Society. IEEE Standard for System Verilog-Unified Hardware Design, Specification, and Verification Language - IEEE 1800-2009. 2009.

[22] Incisive Software Extension Product from Cadence Design System.

[23] Virtual Register Interface Layer over VIPs from Cadence Design System.

[24] Spirit information, http://www.spiritconsortium.org.

[25] Accellera VIP TSC, UVM Register Modeling Requirements, www.accellera.org/activities/vip/

[26] SystemC LRM –IEEE 1666-2005

[27] http://www.techdesignforums.com/practice/guides/transaction-level-modeling-tlm/

[28] www.st.com

[29] www.uvmworld.org

[30] www.SystemVerilog.org

[31] www.ovmworld.org

[32] www.systemc.org

INDEX

www.ingramcontent.com/pod-product-compliance
Lightning Source LLC
Chambersburg PA
CBHW021143070326
40689CB00043B/1111